Naked in
Dream Symbols Revealed

Kathryn & Patrick Andries

OZARK
MOUNTAIN
PUBLISHING

©2014 Kathryn & Patrick Andries

For permission, serialization, condensation, adaptions, or for our catalog of other publications, write to Ozark Mountain Publishing, Inc., P.O. box 754, Huntsville, AR 72740, ATTN: Permissions Department.

Library of Congress Cataloging-in-Publication Data

Andries, Kathryn – 1967 &Andries, Patrick – 1967

Naked in Public: Dream Symbols Revealed by Kathryn & Patrick Andries

This book will assist you in the process by taking you into the depths of your subconscious mind to unravel the process and purpose of dreams. Dream glossary contains over 300 symbols.

1. Dream Symbols 2. Dream Messages 3. Dream Recall 4. Recurring Dreams

1. Andries, Kathryn, 1967; Andries, Patrick 1967 II. Dream Symbols III. Title

Library of Congress Catalog Card Number: 2014941107

ISBN: 9781886940499

Cover Design: enki3d.com

Book set in: Times New Roman, Century Schoolbook

Book Design: Tab Pillar

Published by:

PO Box 754

Huntsville, AR 72740

800-935-0045 or 479-738-2348 fax: 479-738-2448

WWW.OZARKMT.COM

Printed in the United States of America

Endorsement

If you have picked up this book, you are ready to start or expand your journey of consciousness into an understanding of the universality of dreams, as well as develop and apply the personal level of interpretation to your dreams.

Understanding dream symbols can be a confusing task, especially to those new to working with their dreams and also because of the number of dream interpretation books available to the seeker. There are several levels where dreamers dream, and this symbology moves beyond the personal into the realm of the universal. Dreamers seeking insight, guidance and healing through an understanding of their dreams will benefit from this level of insight and discover revelations that can change their perception not only of the night time dream but also of this waking dream and thus become a *see-er*.

The dream exists in the world of the soul, a place between the realm of spirit and this dream of the physical world. When we begin to view our daily physical life more symbolically, we can begin to see larger patterns, themes and tones that run through our dream life and physical daily lives to bring us understanding and healing, as well as provide us with guideposts for living.

Dreamers who work with their dreams begin to see that this world of the physical senses or the "sense" world is as much of a projection as our nightly dream world. As we move into lucid or conscious dreaming, we can begin to interpret our life experiences using dream symbols. This allows us to see how we are creating our lives as we bring that level of conscious awareness into both dream worlds. This is where we begin to recognize that the nightly dream and the daily physical dream are all projections. Sometimes these are described as our "individualistic" dream and our "communal" dream respectively.

Metaphysicians understand that thoughts are things called "thought forms," so who is to say our dream projections, whether our night dreams or our daily living dreams, are not real? Ancient teachings refer to them all as illusions of mind, things we "make," yet we can always use a reminder that our consciousness is limited only by our own beliefs.

The art of dream interpretation is for those who wish to explore that part of their psyche that, as Jung said, lies outside the body in several realms rather than inside the body. Our dreams help us realize that our consciousness is not limited to our physical selves. There are many kinds of dreams. What if they exist in different realms? Understanding the universal nature of symbols is always showing you a deeper meaning. You are the explorer.

Remember that all dreams are about you, the dreamer, and every person, place or thing in a dream is an aspect of you. This makes sense in the realm of understanding that all are one, and there is no separation. The Tibetan Book of the Dead teaches that after we transition from this physical life, we are greeted by demons and angels, and if we but recognize the fearsome and the divine as ourselves, we become enlightened.

The authors of this guide to dream symbols have many years of metaphysical study between them. Through their dream work they have expanded their awareness into a life of conscious living, and the foundation for that is the understanding of universal meanings of dream symbols beyond the personal. Patrick and Kathryn are teachers and explorers who share their wisdom in this book.

I encourage you to use this book in the spirit of discovery and as an art form for your expansion of consciousness on this journey of insight and healing. This book is designed to aid you to understand the universal nature of dream symbols above and beyond the personal meaning that symbols hold.

Kerry Leigh

Table of Contents

Foreword

Patrick and Kathryn Andries were both very curious as children and excited to learn about new things. Kathryn was fascinated by solving puzzles and deciphering codes while Patrick developed an interest in science and music. For Kathryn, this led her to her first love: languages.

Kathryn began to study French and Spanish with great passion and spent time living in France and Spain to deepen her knowledge of those languages and cultures. Gaining insight into different world views, Kathryn came to recognize that language shapes the way that we think and greatly affects culture. Her curiosity eventually led her to incorporate astrology, palmistry and numerology into her puzzle-code repertoire as she learned to decipher the symbols in each of those areas and acquired a great deal of self-knowledge in the process.

Patrick delved into the language of music with equal passion. He was driven by an idea that by developing the use of his mind, he could excel in any area of his choice. Intuitively he began to use the principles of visualization in his musical endeavors which aided him to develop his musical skills. He later applied his interest in science to systematically investigate the abilities of his mind and apply his findings to create greater success in his life.

The study of metaphysics caught their attention, and they began to read and study the subject through a number of different sources. Then they began to study and teach metaphysics at the School of Metaphysics, where they dove into the study of dreams. Dreams occur in a language of symbols, and they found that their respective backgrounds were well-suited for the study. The study of dreams allowed them to go into deeper levels of self-knowledge. This book is the result.

If you wish to probe the richness of your dreams on your journey to self-discovery, this book will serve as an excellent guide.

Kathryn & Patrick Andries
February 2014

CHAPTER 1:
THE NATURE OF DREAMS

The dream is the small hidden door in the deepest and most intimate sanctum of the soul, which opens to that primeval cosmic night that was soul long before there was conscious ego, and will be soul far beyond what a conscious ego could ever reach.

Carl Jung, *The Meaning of Psychology for Modern Man*

THE 5000 YEAR-OLD QUESTION

Throughout history, people have sought the meaning of dreams. The earliest recorded dreams were written on clay tablets by the Mesopotamians. They believed that during dream time the soul left the body and traveled to the places in the dream. Ancient Egyptians recorded dreams in hieroglyphs on papyrus because they believed they were messages from the gods. One of the earliest (1275 B.C.E.) manuscripts on dream interpretation lists dreams, diagnoses ("good" or "bad") and interpretations. Hoping to receive guidance and healing from the gods, Egyptians welcomed the dream state. Priests often acted as dream interpreters; anyone else who could interpret dreams was revered.

Similarly, ancient Greeks believed that gods visited people during the dream state. Hippocrates' (469–399 B.C.E.) theory resonates very closely with our experience that dreams reflect the images the soul[1] experienced during the day. Aristotle

---

[1] *For purposes of this book, we'll define "soul" as the spiritual part of humans, or the subconscious mind.*

1

theorized that dreams could diagnose, as well as predict, illness. In *De insomniis et De divinatione per somnum*, he wrote: "... the most skillful interpreter of dreams is he who has the faculty of absorbing resemblances. I mean that dream presentations are analogous to the forms reflected in water."

Throughout ancient Greece and Rome, hundreds of healing temples (*asclepeions*) offered sanctuary to those who wished to heal through dreams. Priests analyzed dreams, induced a deep state of relaxation and used guided imagery and suggestion to help heal their patients.

In *Oneirocriticon* (*The Interpretation of Dreams*), second-century C.E. Roman author Artemidorus posited that dreams are unique to each person, based on their job, social life and health.

The Mexican culture, as well as indigenous tribes, believed a person could meet up with their ancestors in the dream state.

The darkness and ignorance of the Middle Ages reflected the belief that dreams were evil. Martin Luther spread the fear that the devil could tempt you in your dreams.

Thanks to Sigmund Freud and Carl Jung, a more positive outlook on dreams came to light in the nineteenth century. Freud believed that dreams expressed unfulfilled desires—or those deemed unacceptable by society. Jung emphasized dreams as a way to receive guidance and answers to challenges. He was also instrumental in presenting the idea that people in the dream represent aspects of the dreamer (which coincides with our beliefs).

OUR PERSONAL EXPERIENCE

Dreams are an intuitive experience that almost everyone can relate to. We each dream every night. This has been demonstrated in numerous scientific studies. The issue is remembering our dreams. When we give a little attention to recalling dreams, it is remarkable how quickly the mind responds to the request. This has been demonstrated by hundreds of our students seeking to interpret their dreams. Many students claim not to dream, but with some focused attention on the matter, almost all of them began recording dreams regularly in just a few short weeks.

Dreaming has been a part of every human culture since before the time of recorded history. The discussion of dreams continues back in time to when experiences and traditions were passed on orally. Dreaming is a part of every human experience because the way that our minds function is the same regardless of our culture and background. Just as a doctor can learn how the human body works through the study of one body, with the exception of minor gender differences, we can understand the human mind by examining our own mind. This is one of the greatest gifts of dream interpretation—a deeper understanding of ourselves and each other.

As we begin the quest to understand our dreams, we discover that we are beginning a journey to delve more deeply into understanding ourselves. We begin to see that each dream is reflecting back to us a personal experience. At the same time, understanding our dreams will help us tap into the larger human experience.

When we explore our dreams, we enter into a world that most people never even imagine. It is a world of wonder and delight where anything is possible. There are sometimes frightening events that get our heart racing, or we may even face death. We learn that it is a myth that we die in the waking world if we die in the dream world. Beyond this, we come to realize that the dream world is a metaphor for the waking world in that whatever happens, we are fine.

It is not necessary to believe in the existence of the mind or soul beyond death to interpret our dreams. There is a great deal of value that can be gained from an exploration of dreams on a purely physical level. We do, however, encourage you to keep an open mind to the possibilities ahead, for as we dive more deeply into the subconscious experience, we may find some of our beliefs about ourselves and the world will be shaken to their core. We believe that this is a good thing because it is better to know the truth than to stay trapped in a lie, even if it is a little scary at first.

With this in mind, let us begin this great journey together. Our dreams are the doorway to our minds!

CHAPTER 2:
THE SCIENCE OF DREAMING

Dreams are necessary to life.

—Anaïs Nin

THE BRAIN DURING SLEEP

The level of consciousness during sleep depends on a network of neurons in the brain stem that sends messages to the thalamus, hypothalamus and cerebral cortex. While we sleep, the body reduces the production of adrenaline and corticosteroids and produces human growth hormone (HGH). The pineal gland secretes melatonin, which helps us sleep. Body temperatures and the metabolic rate fall.

Sleep occurs in four[2] stages that may not necessarily occur in sequence: 1) light sleep; 2) slowing heart rate; 3) deep sleep; 4) REM sleep.

NON-RAPID EYE MOVEMENT (NREM) SLEEP

During NREM sleep, there is little or no eye movement. Dreaming rarely occurs. About 40% of the blood flow that normally goes to the brain goes to the muscles. The areas of the brain that relate to language and reasoning experience the–decreased blood flow while the blood flow increases in

---

[2] *Stages of sleep have been reclassified several times, evolving from five to four stages.*

areas of the brain related to processing memories and emotions.

- *Stage 1*: Light sleep with slow eye movement. The brain produces theta waves. This stage lasts 5 to 10 minutes.

- *Stage 2*: The heart rate slows and body temperature drops. There is no eye movement; dreaming seldom occurs. This stage lasts 20 minutes.

- *Stage 3*: Deep sleep. The brain produces delta waves. This is the most common state in which sleepwalking occurs. Dreams may occur.

RAPID EYE MOVEMENT (REM) SLEEP

This is the stage during which most dreaming occurs.

- *Stage 4*: REM sleep occurs in cycles of 90 to 100 minutes and may last 10 to 15 minutes. The time may increase as sleep progresses. The eyes move back and forth rapidly, and muscles relax.

- Depending on how long you sleep, three to four REM cycles may occur each night.

During the REM stage, the brain is quite active. This stage is triggered by the pons, an area of the brain stem that relays nerve impulses between the spinal cord and the brain. The pons signals the body to turn off the motor neurons in the spinal cord, which results in temporary body paralysis—perhaps to stop us from physically responding to dreams. Thought processes are also halted by the pons, which sends signals to the thalamus and the cerebral cortex.

ALCOHOL, DRUGS AND FOOD

Many drugs and alcohol will have an effect on sleep, and hence on dreams. Drugs that interfere with the production of serotonin will negatively affect sleep. We need vitamin B_6, magnesium and vitamin D to convert tryptophan into serotonin. Corticosteroids, such as cortisol and prednisone, interfere with these substances. Drugs that inhibit the transport of calcium, such as benzodiazepines and sleeping pills, interfere with the production of tryptophan. Drugs that affect the thinking process, such as antidepressants will influence dreams.

Some cultures use hallucinogenic drugs to bring people closer to their subconscious. *Ayahuasca* (pronounced ah-*yuh*-**wah**-sk*uh*), a South American plant, has been used by shamans to explore other realms of existence and connect to one's higher self. Ayahuasca causes visual and auditory stimulation and psychological introspection.

Although many people use alcohol to help them sleep, it generally hinders more than helps the sleeping process. Alcohol decreases the amount of REM sleep and increases the amount of NREM sleep. As a result, the length of dream time is reduced. As alcohol is metabolized during the night, the sleeper may experience withdrawal symptoms, such as sweating, awakening and nightmares.[3]

Food affects everything from hormones to blood sugar to neurotransmitters, so watch those late-night snacks. Foods containing the amino acid tryptophan will help induce sleep because the body uses it to make serotonin. Serotonin is a neurotransmitter responsible for slowing nerve impulses to the brain. Calcium also helps the brain use tryptophan to make melatonin, a sleep-inducing hormone. Dairy products contain tryptophan and calcium, and certain carbohydrates contain

---

[3] *Medscape Family Medicine, 2005*

tryptophan (such as cereal with milk, hazelnuts, tofu, peanut butter and tahini sandwiches).

In contrast, protein-rich foods may keep you awake because they contain tyrosine, which stimulates the brain. Eating too heavy a meal late at night can negatively affect sleep. If the body is busy digesting a big meal, you will lose deep sleep due to frequent awakenings and movements (stages 3 and 4, during which a lot of dreaming occurs). Foods and liquids that contain caffeine (chocolate, coffee, etc.) stimulate the brain and may make it difficult to fall asleep or may cause lighter sleep.

CHAPTER 3:
THE METAPHYSICAL PERSPECTIVE

Dreams are the seedlings of reality.

—Napoleon Hill, *Think and Grow Rich*

THE TRINITY OF THE MIND

Throughout this book, we'll refer to different aspects of the mind: the conscious, subconscious and superconscious. They are all interconnected.

- The conscious mind comprises everything that we're aware of. The conscious mind is where attention is focused during the day. We depend on it to perform daily tasks and function in the physical world. The conscious mind continually receives new stimuli and sensory input, which the subconscious mind assimilates during sleep. The conscious mind is the part of our consciousness that works directly with the brain and physical body. To many scientists, this is the only part of the mind. Metaphysics, however, stimulates us to go beyond looking at the physical.

- Just below our conscious perception is the subconscious. Some people believe the subconscious mind is below the conscious mind because the word "sub," means below. When we refer to the subconscious mind being "below" the conscious mind, however, we are referring to what is happening there being below our level of normal awareness. We can become aware of what is happening through techniques like dream interpretation and meditation, but normally we have little indication of what occurs there except for brief flashes of awareness.

The subconscious mind can be a rich source of information and insight. It holds long-term memories and stores understandings. The subconscious mind uses input from the conscious mind to assimilate learning during sleep. It has a much larger memory bank than the conscious mind and stores information and wisdom from past, as well as present lifetimes. The storage capacity of the subconscious mind is infinite. This vast memory bank is often referred to as the Akashic Records or the Book of Life. Some people develop their abilities to the point where they can retrieve past-life memories. One way to do this is through a past life reading. We offer these readings to many people each year. For more information on past life readings, visit www.intuitiveschool.com.

In many different religions there is recognition that there is a part of our consciousness that existed before we were born and continues to exist after the body dies. In the Christian tradition this is called the soul. As we learn to connect with this eternal part of ourselves, we may come to peace with the transition of loved ones, as well as our own mortality. We also gain much deeper insights into the true nature of our existence. Dream interpretation can help us on our journey down this path to self-awareness.

- Our superconscious mind is connected to the force that created us and is the spiritual aspect of the psyche, the "higher self." This is where information about our life purpose is stored. The purpose of life is one of the oldest and deepest questions we ask. There are numerous examples of our attempts to answer this important question, but perhaps the best answers come from our inner self. Our life purpose is imprinted here

10

like the DNA that is in the cells of our bodies. Insights from the superconscious mind help guide us with subtle nudges. The superconscious mind fulfills two roles: 1) it holds the plan for who we are becoming, and 2) it supplies the energy and guidance for us to fulfill that plan.

To use an analogy, we can say that our brain is like a computer. Our personality and beliefs are the software, and the energy of our minds and bodies is like the electricity that enables the computer to run. When the power is on and the programs are running, we experience our lives and all of our thoughts, feelings, actions and reactions. When the power is off, the computer seems dead and lifeless. This is what happens to our brain and physical body when we die. Our consciousness still exists though. All of our experiences are uploaded to the subconscious realm. This is true even in the case of sudden death because there is constant communication between the conscious and subconscious minds. This can be likened to a computer communicating with the Internet.

Our soul or subconscious mind is like a server that we have available for our personal use. In reality our soul is more who we really are than the one little life that we are living now. When one computer on a network dies, the server continues, and we can connect a new computer to our server to begin a new life. We can also install software on the new computer to establish the basic parameters that we desire for our new life.

Our superconscious mind provides the plan and the impetus to fulfill that plan. This plan is not just for one lifetime but for our entire existence that spans all past and future lives and beyond. This is the user of the computer and the network. The user is our true self. When we are able to reach the point where we are aware of being the operator, we will be well on our way to understanding and mastering our mind, consciousness, and dreams.

Dreaming helps replenish energy in our mind. This is done by completing the flow of energy that is initiated when we think. Our thoughts travel to our subconscious mind where the creation process begins. The thought energy moves through our subconscious mind until it manifests in our life as an experience. The experience creates a stimulus that begins the creation process all over again. We are normally aware of our conscious thoughts more than our subconscious thoughts. Dreaming helps us to maintain open lines of communication between the conscious and subconscious minds.

MEDIA AND DREAMS

Media make their way into our dreams through the influence they exert on our conscious mind.

Actors represent what we pretend to be. A preponderance of actors in our dreams suggests that we are losing our true selves to images we identify with. It would be helpful to examine why we are drawn to particular actors, recognize the qualities we want to emulate and begin to develop those qualities. It takes a lot of energy to pretend to be someone other than who we are.

Watching television and movies does not require the use of imagination or willpower because it's a passive exercise. In dreams, this may be embodied by animals. Animals symbolize our habitual behaviors when we simply "go through the motions" without imagination or innovation. Over time our ability to visualize and create can diminish.

What we see on television and in movies may influence and trigger thoughts and emotions that filter into our dreams. Our subconscious mind will use recently viewed symbols to make a point. After viewing a frightening movie that features a dragon, we might have a nightmare with a dragon, rather than a monster, to represent a fear we cannot control.

CHAPTER 4:
UNDERSTANDING DREAMS

In dreams no one wears a mask.

—Edward Counsel

WHY INTERPRET DREAMS?

Everything we do creates mental patterns, some of which set up negative emotions. Self-criticism may lead to negativity and sorrow; worrying may create fear. A pattern of appreciation may result in happiness and contentment.

Dreaming is a way to assimilate the input, stimuli, thoughts and attitudes experienced during the day. It allows our conscious and subconscious minds to communicate with us through images. Lack of sleep (and the resulting assimilation) makes many of us irritable. In fact, sleep research shows that when we are deprived of sleep, we may hallucinate as a way for our mind to assimilate our experiences.

We all dream even though we may not remember our dreams. By age 60, we have spent about 20 years sleeping, and more than two and a half years dreaming. There is much to be gained by exploring this significant part of our lives.

Dreams are messages from our subconscious mind that reflect thoughts and attitudes about the previous day. They reveal moods and emotions. It's up to us to recognize and respond to them.

BENEFITS OF DREAM INTERPRETATION

There are many benefits from learning how to decode our dreams. Here are a few:

- Dreams may help us understand our life purpose.

- Dreams indicate whether we are in harmony with our life purpose.

- Dreams indicate our state of spiritual, mental, emotional, and physical health.

- Dreams increase our self-awareness.

- Our subconscious mind will accurately reflect the truth about our thoughts and feelings.

- Dreams help us become aware of our personality characteristics and thinking patterns.

- Dreams may offer us insights into how we see our world.

- Dreams aid in problem-solving and creativity. Mary Shelley used information from the dream state to write *Frankenstein*. Einstein attributes his insights on the theory of relativity to his dreams. Thomas Edison frequently used dreams to resolve challenges with his inventions.

- Dreams can show us potential events (precognitive dreams).

- Understanding our dreams may bring us peace of mind, focus and concentration as we identify what is important.

- Meditations will deepen.

- We may break our cause-and-effect (karmic) patterns.

- We may raise our energy level to a higher vibration, resulting in a greater sense of inner peace and contentment.

HOW TO INTERPRET DREAMS

The first step to interpreting our dreams is understanding how to decode symbols.

STEP ONE: DECODING DREAM SYMBOLS

In conversation, we use words to form images. When we examine the words that we use, we will find that there is an image behind every word. The mind flashes an image and then chooses an appropriate word to describe that image. We have become so accustomed to using words that we seldom realize the process that is occurring. If we close our eyes and picture a car, we can once again see the image associated with the word "car." It's important to remember that the word "car" means all cars and not just the one that we are visualizing. We have a file marked "car" that has images of all possible cars we can imagine in it. When we listen to someone speak, the process is reversed so that we hear the word and then associate an image with it. Is it any wonder that we have so many communication challenges in life? When we see a car in our mind, it may not be anything like the car that the person talking to us is seeing in his or her mind.

In dreams, the subconscious mind speaks to us in pictures. What we need to learn in relation to dreams is the language that is being used. Almost everyone recognizes a picture of a bird, yet if someone says *pajaro*, only Spanish-speaking people would understand. Language allows us to translate and communicate the pictures in our minds. With dreams we need to understand the context. The dream is relating what is occurring in our mind, so we need to look at the information in that context. One way to do this is to look at the function of the image. How is it used in our life?

15

Dream language is based on the function of the symbol. A symbol is generally any noun (person, place, or thing) in the dream. The conscious mind understands the literal meaning of things; dreams relate the figurative function of these things. When we interpret a dream, we must think about the function of things in our dreams in relation to our bodies or life. For example, the function of a car is to transport us from one place to another. What transports our consciousness from one place to another? The body. Its function is similar to that of a car; therefore, a car in a dream represents the body. The function of food is to nourish our bodies, and knowledge nourishes our minds. Thus, food in a dream represents knowledge.

STEP TWO: PUTTING THE EMPHASIS ON US

The second step to interpreting dreams involves putting the emphasis on us! The main concept to understand is that every dream centers on the dreamer. Dreams reflect thoughts and attitudes and interactions with others and the world. Every person, place and thing in a dream represents an aspect of the dreamer. The dream is coming from our mind, so we must remember that it is all about us. Sometimes people have related getting angry at someone because of what happened in a dream. This dream image was created because of some relationship to the person in the dream and has no reflection on the actual person.

STEP THREE: WRITING THE DREAM IN A NOTEBOOK

The third step to interpreting dreams is to write the dream in a journal or notebook. Write down the dream in as much detail as possible. It is best to write down the dream as soon as we are awake. The longer that we wait; the more likely it is that we will forget information from the dream. It is also possible to add in things that were not originally there.

STEP FOUR: UNDERLINING IMPORTANT SYMBOLS

Next we must underline all the important symbols in our dream. Important symbols would be people, places, things and action words.

STEP FIVE: WRITING DEFINITIONS OF SYMBOLS

In the far right column or above each symbol—this requires you to skip lines—write the definition of each symbol. Start by looking up the symbols in the glossary at the back of this book. It would take a very large dictionary to cover every possible symbol, and symbols can vary in meaning due to context, so the ultimate goal is to learn to understand the language of dreams so that we can translate the symbols for ourselves.

STEP SIX: COMBINING SYMBOLS & WRITING INTERPRETATIONS

Now combine the symbols and write an interpretation of the dream. Just like learning a foreign language, putting the symbols together allows you to get the message. Once you have the main picture of the dream put together, look in your life for where this dream may apply. Remember that the dream is referring to your thoughts and feelings during the day. Resist the urge to take the dream literally as you are interpreting and applying it.

STEP SEVEN: APPLYING THE DREAM TO YOUR LIFE

Once we identify where this dream applies in our life, we can decide how we are going to use this information to improve ourselves and our lives. Remember that the purpose of learning to interpret our dreams is to increase our self-awareness. The purpose of increasing our self-awareness is to better ourselves and our life. Once we see what is happening in our life, we can make some changes and see how our dreams change!

WHO ARE WE?

Who are the main characters in the dream? People in a dream represent how we view ourselves, as well as our thinking patterns. When we use associative thinking (free association)[4] to identify the first descriptor that comes to mind about someone in our dream, this descriptor/adjective is an aspect of ourselves that we brought out the previous day. For example, a dream about a neighbor, who we think of as funny, represents a humorous aspect of our personality. We can even think of a second word that describes the person in the dream. For example, we may describe a woman in our dream as kind and reserved. This could indicate a part of our personality where we are generally nice to people but tend to hold back in giving too much of ourselves. Unfamiliar people indicate there are parts of us that we don't know or understand. If these unfamiliar people continue to appear in our dreams, there may be a need for self- reflection.

What about gender? Dreaming of men and women reveals how we see our masculine and feminine sides. Are the men in our dreams big, domineering or aggressive? Intellectual or introspective? Gentle, sexy or weak? How are the women portrayed?

In general we can describe most men as displaying aggressive tendencies. This is not to say that all men fight all of the time, but rather looking at the aggressive quality as an outpouring of energy. This tendency goes back in evolutionary terms to men tending to be the hunters in the community. The needs that developed were to go out, sometimes for long periods of time, living in the wild. There was often a need to defend against other predators. When the prey was located, it may have required a period of high exertion to bring it down. Then the animal had to be carried back to the community. This all

---

[4] *Associative thinking may be used to come up with descriptors for cities and other objects as well as for people. The use of associative thinking helps understand dreams at a deeper level.*

required the expenditure of large amounts of energy. The men who were stronger, faster, and smarter tended to be more successful, lived longer and produced more offspring.

The female energy by comparison is described as being more receptive. The receptive energy is open to what is available. While the men tended go out to hunt, the women stayed closer to home to gather resources. They may have gathered berries and nuts that were available and tended to survival needs for shelter and preparation of food to eat. The females also developed innate skills for caring for others. This nurtured the receptive energies as they cared for the young and old of the community. Once again, those females who were more successful tended to have more children who survived to reproduce.

It is not accurate to say that men are aggressive only and women are receptive only. In reality it is more like tipping a scale in one direction or another. We could say that most men are 51% aggressive and 49% receptive. On the other hand, women could be 51% receptive and 49% aggressive. Some men and women may exhibit a stronger or weaker tendency than normal. We each need a balance of aggressive and receptive energy to function in our lives. If women had no aggressive tendencies, they would never get out of bed in the morning. Likewise, if men had no receptive ability, they could never observe their environment, listen to their intuition—or listen to anyone else for that matter.

WHAT'S HAPPENING?

What happens in the dream? What are the characters doing? Action reveals your focus. A dream of preparing food, for example, means that attention is focused on knowledge. Food represents knowledge because when we look at the function of food, it provides nourishment for our bodies. Since the dream is coming from the perspective of the mind, we need to look at what nourishes our minds. In this case knowledge feeds the mind. Food then symbolizes knowledge and preparing food is giving attention to knowledge.

WHERE ARE WE?

Where does the dream take place? Place also represents our focus. A dream in a church means that attention is focused on spirituality. Again, the function of a church is to give attention to our spirituality. It may also be seen as a place to experience spiritual community. Some other common locations include: home—this is where we live, so it is normally described as being the mind; work—this is where we achieve our sustenance and our goals; school—this is where we give attention to learning; a restaurant—this is giving attention to taking in knowledge and making it a part of ourselves.

HOW'S IT GOING?

How are the characters acting? Are they anxious, happy, rushed or bored? This component reflects the dreamer's emotions and state of mind. If a character is happy in the dream, the dreamer's state of mind is one of happiness.

Dream symbols may be understood at three levels: universal, cultural, and personal. Let's examine these.

- *__Universal__*: A universal symbol is one that does not differ from culture to culture or person to person. Everyone needs air, water and food to survive. In a dream air represents thought; food represents knowledge; water represents emotional life experience. We are all sharing the experience of being human, so there are many universal experiences in life. In truth, we share far more similarities than differences.

- *__Cultural__*: Culture[5] may influence what dream images symbolize. In some parts of the world it may be more

---

[5] *Note that this book uses the culture of the United States as its frame of reference to interpret dreams and dream symbols.*

common to travel by ox cart than by car. In this case the ox cart would represent the physical body. Look at the cultural significance of the symbol to see if the meaning might change. In the previous example the universal aspect of the ox cart is that it is a vehicle, and vehicles represent the physical body.

- ***Personal***: We may have an emotional attachment or a unique relationship to a particular symbol. As a child we may have had a near drowning experience and so have a very strong reaction to being in or near water. Someone who restores old cars may have a special meaning assigned to certain cars when they show up in dreams. We will usually know when we have a personal meaning attached to a symbol because there will be a strong thought or feeling associated with it.

Our recommendation is to always begin with the universal aspect of the symbol. At the core of the symbol this universal aspect will still exist. Next, if there is a special cultural or personal significance we can look at how that may affect the meaning of the symbol for us. As we mentioned earlier, it will usually be apparent when there is added meaning to a symbol.

DREAMS AND LIFE PURPOSE

Life purpose involves learning to love oneself and others, developing and sharing talents and working through lessons. Dreams reveal the degree to which we are living our life purpose.[6] In dreams, harmonious relationships indicate loving parts of ourselves. Fighting with others reveals an unloving attitude toward ourselves. Conflicts with people in our dreams may offer clues to the lessons we face.

---

[6] *For more detailed information on life purpose and the Discover Your Life Purpose Course, visit http://www.discoveryourlifepurpose.org/ or www.kathrynandries.com.*

The function of our hands is to create. We use our hands with virtually everything that we do to interact with and manipulate our environment; thus, in a dream, hands represent purpose. What is it that we are creating in our life? What is our motivation or benefit for creating it? It's important to notice what our hands are doing to determine the extent to which we are following our purpose in life. An animal biting our hand may indicate that there is a pattern of thought or behavior that is interfering with our purpose.

Dreams of a sexual nature represent the ability to create and develop our gifts and talents. They show the harmony among various aspects of our personality, necessary for any creation. Sex allows procreation to occur. Just as a couple can create offspring through sex, we may have signs in our dreams of a new part of our personality being created. If we like to write and play music, for example, we might see these two parts of self come together to create a new aspect, maybe a newfound interest in songwriting.

A nightmare reveals a challenge that is overpowering and out of our control (and, most likely, not in alignment with our purpose). When a nightmare occurs, we need to pay close attention. This normally indicates that a change needs to occur in our consciousness.

Precognitive dreams can offer insights into the next step toward fulfilling our life purpose. Precognition is the ability of the mind to perceive an event before it happens. We will need to go much further into the structure of the mind to understand how this occurs, but one way to look at this is that all events occur as the result of choices and forces that have already been set into motion. Our mind knows, for example, that our body is fighting off a foreign invader and sets our immune system into high gear long before we experience any physical symptoms. So, too, our mind can follow the thoughts of others, as well as forces in nature, to perceive an event before it develops in the physical world. When we learn to recognize these dreams and interpret them accurately, we can use this valuable information to understand the choices that are before us and make the best decisions for our growth and well-being. These informed decisions will often be in alignment with our life purpose.

OUR BODY, THE CAR

As stated earlier, a car represents the body. The condition of the car reflects the condition of our body: a broken car indicates that it is time to heal our body. Car parts correspond to certain body parts. Use the rule of function to determine which car parts relate to which body parts:

- Brakes slow a car and relate to the nervous system and the need to slow down in our life.

- Do we need an oil change? If so, our joints may be getting stiff and need lubrication.

- Gas is the fuel that allows a car to move; this corresponds to the amount of energy we have. If we are out of gas, it is time to refuel and recharge. Sleep and/or food may be needed.

- Hoses represent veins and arteries. Are things flowing smoothly or are the hoses (arteries) blocked or broken?

- How we drive our car shows us how we use our body to get through life. If we are stuck in traffic, for example, there may be some blocks in our ability to move forward in our life.

- A car crash indicates that our body is not in balance and needs healing. It also represents a loss of control.

HOW ARE WE MOVING THROUGH LIFE?

In our dreams we may find ourselves travelling by car, boat, or airplane. These different modes of transportation reflect what we are using to move forward in life. A car shows we are using our physical body to maneuver through life. A boat reveals we are using our emotions to propel us through life. An airplane reveals we are using our thoughts to move through life.

We can take this a step further by looking at the speed of the vehicle. An airplane is a fast vehicle. It relates to thought, which is the fastest way to move forward. When we try to fulfill a goal using only our physical abilities, it can take much longer. It may take only a moment to decide that we want to become a homeopathic doctor and become excited about it, but it will take years of study to realize this dream. Thus, our experiences in life move slower than our thoughts or emotions.

OUR MIND, THE HOUSE

A house represents the mind. (According to the function rule, a house is where we physically live; our mind is where our consciousness lives.) The state of the house reflects the state of our mind. For example, an elegant mansion reflects someone with high self-esteem who likely engages in positive thinking. A rundown shack reflects someone with low self-esteem, who likely engages in negative thinking.

Each room in a house represents a different part of the mind:

- Kitchen: where we prepare knowledge to be received;

- Dining Room: where we take in knowledge to make it a part of our learning.

- Bedroom: a place to rest, recharge and assimilate our experiences

- Bathroom: where we release unwanted thoughts and feelings.

- Living room: the primary area of activity and learning in our life.

TYPES OF DREAMS

Some dreams represent thoughts common to most of us, such as the desire to get ahead in life, feeling out of control, and fearing change. Although the dream symbols may differ, these dreams may be experienced by members of any culture.

Nightmares reflect a state of fear in our waking life. We usually feel out of control and are having difficulty directing our life. Fears may have to do with unfulfilled desires. Children may absorb the fears of adults in their lives. A small child may experience fear simply because of the newness of everything. Some children may feel a lack of control if adults make all the decisions for them. (These children could benefit by making more of their own decisions.)

Often a nightmare is the result of a series of dreams that have gone unheeded. When we look back through the dream journals of students who report nightmares, we often find that the theme of the nightmare showed up several times before. The students had the opportunity to address these concerns but did not. The images and activity of the dreams became more graphic and intense until they were finally reported as nightmares. What began as a relatively benign dream developed into a nightmare. This is likened to a parent struggling to capture the attention of a child. If the child still fails to respond, the parent may continue to raise the voice until the child finally pays attention. Likewise, the subconscious mind will repeatedly attempt to communicate important information and escalate the intensity if it is an important change that needs to occur.

Flying dreams are pleasurable because they give us a sense of freedom. These dreams indicate we are a freethinker who does not allow dogma or other limitations to stop us from accomplishing our goals. People proficient in spiritual disciplines, such as meditation and astral projection[7] may

---

[7] *Astral projection is the ability to consciously leave our body and direct our attention elsewhere, such as to another physical location.*

25

experience flying dreams, indicative of their ability to separate from the body when awake. When we desire to experience flying dreams, we focus on our ability to create whatever we desire in our life. When we realize that our mind is a creative device that will create whatever image we hold in mind, we will come to know that not even the sky is the limit!

Dreams of nudity reflect an attitude of openness and honesty in the dreamer's waking life. If we are embarrassed by our nakedness and are running for cover, we may have revealed more about our true self than we are comfortable with during the previous day. We may have confided in someone and regretted our openness. When we are naked, there is nothing to hide. This can often leave us feeling exposed and vulnerable. If we are comfortable being naked, then we are at ease being honest with ourselves and others.

Recurring dreams indicate that we are repeating a behavior and may not be causing a necessary change in our life. The subconscious mind is repeating the message so that it can be acted upon. If the dream goes unheeded for an extended period of time and the message is important to us, then the recurring dream may become a nightmare to get our attention. As mentioned earlier, this is like a parent yelling at a child to get the child's attention. Pay attention to the message and take action, and the dream will change or cease.

School dreams are a common recurring dream in many cultures where people send their children to school. The school dream, in general, is a dream about learning the lessons of life. What occurs in the dream will indicate how we handle life's lessons and how prepared we feel to address a learning opportunity in our life. For example, we may be late for class or can't find the right classroom. Or, worse yet, we arrive in class only to find it is test day, and we are not prepared. This dream means that we feel unprepared to meet life's challenges. An exam in a dream is an evaluation of ourselves to see where we are compared to where we want to be.

Death in a dream indicates that a change is taking place within ourselves. The degree to which we are afraid of change in our waking life is the degree to which we fear death in the dream. A person who dies in a dream is an aspect of the dreamer that is changing or has changed. Murder is a forced change, which is why it is frightening in a dream. When we have this type of dream, we feel helpless in our life. We feel that changes in our life are out of our control and being forced upon us. If we have this kind of dream, we remind ourselves that change is a natural part of life and that we determine how we change by the thoughts that we choose.

Precognitive dreams may show possible future events. Precognitive dreams are perhaps one of the most mystical aspects of dream interpretation. They are often misunderstood and difficult to reproduce. Precognitive dreams are usually more vivid and intense than other dreams, and the events will occur in waking life exactly as they did in the dream. In precognitive dreams all of the events will be true to life. In other words, there will not be any segments with flying or walking on clouds or any other event that would not occur in our waking life.

With experience, we can begin to distinguish this type of dream from others. What we do with the information received is our choice. If it is a good dream, there are usually no reservations about sharing the information with everyone concerned. However, if the dream is negative, we need to use our best judgment regarding the communication. One thing to keep in mind about precognitive dreams is that all future events are dependent upon our current choices and the choices of those in the dream. If we have a precognitive dream about meeting another person, and we make a different choice or the other person makes a different choice, then the meeting will not come to pass.

Our ability to make different choices is a powerful tool we can use should we dream of an undesirable event. It is a good idea not to assume a dream is precognitive, because these dreams tend to be rare. Until we have more experience with identifying precognitive dreams, it is advisable to interpret a dream we suspect to be precognitive just like we would a normal dream. Over time you will learn to recognize these prophetic dreams.

Running dreams occur when we are trying to run from someone or something in the dream. It indicates that we are avoiding or running away from some aspect of ourselves. We may tend to procrastinate and have had several people point this out to us, yet we don't want to take a serious look at this issue. In this example, we may have a person show up in our dream that represents this tendency to procrastinate, and we are trying to avoid this person.

Sometimes we may find that as we are attempting to make our escape that our legs are moving in slow motion, and it feels like we are running in molasses. This indicates that our consciousness has shifted from one state to another, but we have not adjusted to this shift. When we have this type of dream, we can identify the aspect that we are avoiding and confront this within ourselves. We can also relax and slow our thinking to allow us to adjust to the shift that is occurring in our consciousness. In other dreams where we are running and getting nowhere, we may have run around all day with no goal or purpose for our activity. We may feel unfocused, scattered and thwarted from making progress. In this case we would benefit from setting goals and visualizing.

Sexual dreams represent creation occurring in our consciousness. Sex allows for the potential of procreation in life and has a similar effect in the dream state, except that it is more about creating with thought. Sex is not only used for procreation in waking life, but is also used to become intimate with a partner. A sex dream in this context can represent harmony occurring between aspects of our selves. The sex partner represents the aspect of our personality that we are using to create something, or it may indicate where greater harmony and intimacy is developing. Creating involves using the conscious and subconscious minds in tandem; this cooperation creates the pleasure and harmony we associate with sex. The blending of male and female energies also represents the balance of the aggressive and receptive energies that represent the dynamic dance of creation. This is represented in Taoism by the yin yang symbol.

Visitations. A deceased person may appear in a dream. The souls of the deceased (the part of us that exists beyond the death of the physical body) can contact us easily while we sleep. During sleep, the conscious mind quiets the day's mental chatter and allows the subconscious mind to communicate with other souls. During a visitation, the deceased person in the dream will send thoughts of comfort or an important message. Often the deceased person will be seen just standing over us and smiling. If a message is given, it will be through telepathy. The deceased person's thoughts will be heard in the mind, and the lips of the deceased will not move. There is no air in the dream state and so there is no need to use the voice and mouth. If the person in the dream is using the mouth to speak, then this is a symbol to represent an aspect of our selves and is not a visitation.

BE AN EFFECTIVE DREAM INTERPRETER

We may wish to help others understand their dreams due to our fascination with them. To be a successful dream interpreter, it would be helpful to have expertise in the following:

- We must be familiar with and be able to interpret the symbolic language of the mind based on the function model presented in this book.

- We will need expertise in putting the symbols together to see the message. Simply relating the meaning of isolated symbols may help—or confuse.

- We must interpret our own dreams and apply their messages to our life. When we master this skill (the time needed to do so varies from person to person), we will be ready to help someone else.

- We must be able to use our intuition to see the big picture and to understand the dream at a deeper level. Intuition will help us make connections and gain insights.

When we begin to interpret dreams, we will most likely need the assistance of a dream interpretation expert to verify our interpretations and/or offer further insights. It's simply part of the learning process.

A skilled dream interpreter does not need to know the client. We have successfully interpreted dreams of strangers from foreign countries. However, it may be helpful to know a client to apply cultural and personal meanings to dream symbols. For example, if we did not know that our client was a zookeeper, we would offer the standard interpretation of his/her dream about working with animals (habits). If we knew, however, we would incorporate the special significance of animals and interpret the dream as an effort to set and achieve the client's goals, because a place of work is where we achieve goals in our lives.

To avoid potential inaccuracies, we ask our clients about their professions and countries of origin. This allows us to account for cultural and personal connections to a symbol. Identical dreams experienced by different people may not have the same meaning. The interpreter must consider cultural and personal differences in the meaning of dream symbols.

CHAPTER 5:
MANAGING DREAMS

Between the dreams of night and day there is not so great a difference.

—Carl Jung, *Psychology of the Universe*

INGESTED SUBSTANCES AND DREAMS

Sleep blocks stimuli, such as light and noise, and frees us to focus on the subconscious mind. In addition to such stimuli experienced during the day, food, drink and other ingested substances may affect our dreams.

Eating a heavy meal at dinner or indulging in a late-night snack may make it more difficult to release the attention from the body and conscious mind. Time that could be spent with the subconscious mind is used to address bodily needs, such as bathroom use, digestion, etc. The first meal of the day is called "break-fast" because we are breaking the fast of the previous night while we were sleeping. When the body is freed from the process of digestion, it is easier to quiet the conscious mind and focus on the subconscious mind. As a general health practice, it is good to stop eating at least one hour before going to sleep. This helps us enter into a deep restful sleep with productive dream time.

Alcohol influences the dream state, just as it does the waking state. We are less likely to remember dreams after drinking. Drinking causes us to maintain focus in the conscious state; therefore, receiving messages from the subconscious becomes more difficult. Dreams may reflect the reason for drinking. Drinking to escape sadness or other emotional pain may result in dreams populated with sad people or painful events. Celebratory drinking may bring about dreams with happy people and enjoyable events. Drinking impairs the thinking process, so our head may appear damaged in a dream. Alcohol will impair the strength of the will over time just as it impairs the reasoning ability. We create our lives with our thoughts. When our ability to use our reasoning to choose our thoughts is impaired through alcohol or drug use, our mind becomes like a ship without a rudder. We begin to float aimlessly in life.

Some drugs may allow access to images and messages from the subconscious. However, using drugs over time may inhibit learning to connect with the inner self and encourage dependency. Ancient Greeks and Dionysian cults used drugs to enhance their dreams. Priestesses at Delphi chewed leaves to enter a trance-like state during which they received divinatory messages. Australian aborigines use *pituri* to lead them into a dream state. Other cultures have also used native hallucinogenic plants to enhance dreams and induce altered states of consciousness. Asians used opium; Mexicans use peyote and seeds from the Mexican morning glory.[8]

CINEMA THERAPY

Cinema therapy may be used to elicit a specific mood or feeling. For example, watching an uplifting movie while depressed may bring about a happier mood. In addition, it may influence dreams because the visual and auditory elements can be powerful enough to cause a shift in mood and thinking.

Since our dreams are a reflection of our thoughts and attitudes about the previous day, movies can greatly affect our dreams. We can use movies to help us make a shift in our thinking or get us out of a funk. Movies can cause us to forget our own thoughts and focus on what is happening with the characters in the movie. If you want to feel more positive, choose uplifting and inspiring movies. If you want to feel more loving, choose a romantic movie. There are several cinema therapy books which list movies according to their genre. Two good books are

---

[8] *Cohen, Daniel. Dreams, Visions, & Drugs: A Search for Other Realities. New York: New Viewpoints, 1977.*

Cinematherapy: The Girl's Guide to Movies for Every Mood and *Reel Spirit.*

RESPONDING TO YOUR DREAMS

Dreams are the result of two-way communication between our conscious and subconscious minds. Our conscious mind transfers what we have experienced during the day to the subconscious mind. During dreamtime our subconscious mind then sends messages to our conscious mind about how we have integrated those experiences into our consciousness as learning.

The mind speaks in symbols to us continuously through people, events, actions and emotions, giving us direction and advice and showing us events about to manifest. To respond to these dream messages, we can develop our will and pay attention to our dream symbols.

After we have interpreted each dream, we form a suggestion or affirmation for our day and follow through with it. If we dream about being hungry and not being able to find food, for example, we will recall that food is information that can become knowledge. If we had this dream, we might decide to conduct research on a topic via the library, Internet, or other sources.

We will also need to make the necessary changes in our life. For example, eliminate and change victim thoughts so our mind will be more serene. A nightmare in which a monster is chasing us reveals that we feel things happening to us that are out of our control. We can change this sense of being victimized with the affirmation, "I am the creator of my life, and I can create anything that I desire." We can repeat this ten times a day. Yogis refer to acting on the messages provided by dreams as "dream alchemy."

DAYDREAMING, LUCID DREAMING AND SLEEPWALKING

DAYDREAMING

When we daydream, the mind wanders and accesses the subconscious mind. This state allows us to receive intuitive input and expand our imagination. It is very common to receive an answer to a question or an important insight when we are doing something mundane, like washing dishes or mowing the lawn. When we are doing these activities, we have a simple and singular focus. As our conscious mind maintains a relaxed focus, we can access the intuitive mind. It is necessary to be focused on positive thoughts because when we are focused on doubt and worry, we shut down our intuitive abilities.

Most daydreams are of a pleasant nature. We may dream of an ideal encounter with another person, a special trip to an exotic locale, or maybe what it would be like if we had more money than we could possibly spend. Regardless of what our daydreams are, the action of maintaining that relaxed focus in our conscious mind allows us to access our intuitive abilities. We can learn to use our daydreaming in a productive way by incorporating our desires into them. We can keep a list of our top ten or twelve desires handy so that we remember what they are. When we find ourselves in a position to be able to safely daydream, we direct our dreaming toward imaging what our life will be like when we have received one or more of those desires. We can be aware of what comes to mind that may be an answer to how we can create that desire. As we learn to do this, we will be developing a very important skill of the mind called *visualization*.

LUCID DREAMING

Lucid dreaming allows us to bring our conscious awareness to the subconscious mind during our dream time. With practice, we may learn to direct the dream and interact with the dream symbols. For example, if we are having a dream where we are being chased, we may choose to stop running, turn around and face our pursuer. At this point we can ask what this person or animal represents. Remember that anything is possible in a dream. We can even talk to our car if that comes to mind. As we develop this ability, we can learn much more from our dream experiences.

One important lesson is that we cannot be harmed during our dreamtime. When we really know this, our dreamtime experiences will be very different. The more that we discover about our dreamtime and delve into this magical place in mind, the more we will discover and realize the true nature of the world that we live in. One important note, however, is to refrain from making changes to our dreams until we understand what the symbols actually mean in our life. We must remember that every person, place and thing in our dream represents an aspect of us, so we should treat our dream symbols with kindness.

One interesting story about lucid dreaming comes from Susan, a student of dream interpretation who was learning about and practicing the art of lucid dreaming. Susan had a recurring dream about a dark man who was pursuing her through dimly lit streets at night. Through interpreting her dreams, she knew that he represented a part of herself that she was apprehensive about, but she was never able to identify what part of herself that was. She also knew that the darkness in the dream represented her lack of awareness on this subject. She decided to put her new skill to work and when she successfully gained conscious awareness in the dream, the next time that she had that dream she stopped running and stood her ground. Carefully, she controlled her emotions as her pursuer caught up to her. As he came into the light, she could finally see his face but did not recognize him, so she asked, "Who are you and what do you represent for me?" He answered back without hesitation, "I represent your sense of low self-esteem."

Everything became clear for her at that point, and she began right away to change those thoughts in her mind. She never had that dream again.

Another story comes from Stephen. He was a runner and also learning the art of dream interpretation and lucid dreaming. In his recurring dream he was being pursued by a tiger. Upon interpreting his dream, he considered the tiger to be a habit that may be harmful to him. Being mindful of his health, he wanted to change this habit. The next time that he had the dream, he produced a spear and killed the tiger. The next morning he went for his usual run and found that he had difficulty finding his rhythm. He felt like he was learning how to run all over again. He lacked the pace and endurance that he had developed. Looking at his interpretation again with his teacher, he realized that the tiger was not harmful to him but actually represented his habit of running. The tiger kept him motivated and symbolized the stamina and vitality that he gained from running, as well as the feeling that he could take on the world afterwards. By killing the tiger in his dream, he had disrupted this pattern in his mind. Fortunately, due to his years of experience, it only took about two weeks for him to develop his pace again. He also learned a valuable lesson about changing a symbol before he knew what it represented in his life.

SLEEPWALKING AND SLEEP-TALKING

Sleepwalking (somnambulism) and sleep-talking (somniloquy) may occur when a dreamer does not release worries and concerns from the conscious mind before bedtime. Loud noises, a full bladder and other factors may also trigger these behaviors. During dream time the body releases a chemical that naturally inhibits movement. In the cases of sleepwalking and sleep-talking, this natural protective mechanism is overridden. This allows movement and speech during sleep. Sleepwalking occurs during Stage 3 of Non-rapid eye movement (NREM) sleep when we are in deep sleep and still have muscle control. We are not acting out dream scenarios at this level of sleep. Sleep-talking usually occurs during NREM sleep. In this case usually we are verbalizing conscious mind worries and concerns. If it occurs during rapid eye movement (REM) sleep, the dreamer speaks aloud words occurring in the dream. Speech is usually clearer during NREM sleep.

In both instances, we usually don't remember the event upon awakening. Relaxing before bed, perhaps with a shower and meditation, may help stop these behaviors.

THE EFFECT ON RELATIONSHIPS

Dreams may improve relationships, especially the most important one: that with our inner self. Dreams bring greater self-awareness, which may also help improve relationships with others. Since everyone in the dream represents an aspect of us, we can learn about our qualities and the ways we express them. We can also learn how we feel about ourselves, based on interactions with others in our dreams. We may learn about our desires, the way we use our creativity, and much more.

When we know ourselves well, we can choose our most suitable partners and friends. Lack of self-awareness may create confusion and problems in relationships as people tend to project their issues onto each other. The self-aware dreamer is less likely to project issues.

Dream interpretation may help us gain insights into relationship challenges, deepen our understanding of others and perhaps receive guidance. Discussion of dreams is a quick way to bypass superficial conversation and can be quite fun. Couples therapy with a trained dream interpreter may bring to light the deeper issues facing each person.

A student of ours lived in fear for several years due to her recurring dreams of her husband being intimate with other women. This led to suspicion. Her lack of trust was hurting their relationship. When she learned that the dream mistresses were aspects of herself, she sighed with relief, regretted the years of worry and apologized to her husband with a 10-day cruise to Alaska.

DREAM INCUBATION

Dream incubation is a technique to focus the mind on a specific issue or topic, perhaps to receive guidance or solve problems. Albert Einstein often used dreams to receive work-related insights. Thomas Edison was also well-known for taking short naps in his lab to use dream time to produce solutions to problems that he faced with inventions. Here are six easy steps we can use to begin using dream incubation in our life:

1. Before going to sleep, focus on the problem or issue we need help with.

2. Write down exactly what we want to learn about the issue. This can be done in our dream journal.

3. Relax before going to sleep.

4. Have confidence in our dreams.

5. Refer to the "Enhancing Dream Recall" section in Chapter 5 to increase the chances of remembering our dreams. (We are more likely to remember a dream if we awake mid-dream; some people set an alarm for 3:00 or 4:00 a.m. in hopes of catching a dream in mid-stream.)

6. Once we recall the dream, interpret it symbolically and consider other ways that it can bring us a solution to our question or issue.

OUR DREAM DOCTOR

Early detection of an illness is key to successful recuperation. Dreams show thinking patterns that could lead to physical problems. Stress, a major culprit in many physical disorders, may reveal itself in dreams as conflicts with people, arriving late to school or being unprepared for a test. Many feel stressed when they awake from such a dream. Recurring nightmares are also a sign of stress buildup. Getting to the root of our stress allows us to make changes before it causes permanent damage.

Some dreams have an emotional tone that may lead to health disorders. Extreme sadness may indicate depression; extreme hate, especially self-hatred, may lead to cancer. We can examine the emotions in our dreams and trace them back to the thoughts that caused them. It is often easier to recognize emotions than thoughts. Louise Hay in her book *Heal Your Body*, further explores the connection between thoughts, emotions and disease.

Our dreams may show a part of our body that needs healing. The aspect of us that knows how to heal may appear as a doctor or other type of healer, like a shaman, and offer advice on healing.

ENHANCING DREAM RECALL

Many things can interfere with dream recall. An overactive mind consumed with worry may be the biggest stumbling block to remembering dreams. An extremely busy life can pull all our attention into the conscious mind, leaving no room for messages from our subconscious.

These steps are designed to enhance dream recall:

1. We should dedicate a notebook and pen to record our dreams and keep them at the side of our bed. This helps to establish our commitment to dream recall and interpretation. As this commitment becomes impressed

upon our mind, we will find that our dream recall improves and becomes more consistent.

2. Our subconscious mind always responds to our needs and desires, so cultivating a desire to remember our dreams will help us do so. Before going to bed, say aloud, "I will remember my dreams," and then write this down in your dream notebook at the top of the page. Our desire will increase once we begin to interpret our dreams and see the wisdom they offer us.

3. When we use our five senses to practice focusing our attention during the day on everything we do and on the people we encounter, our awareness in the dream state will be enhanced.

4. We can cultivate our internal alarm clock so that we can awaken naturally and relaxed rather than be jarred awake by an alarm clock. The loud buzz of alarm clocks tends to jolt our consciousness into wakefulness, causing us to forget our dreams. If we are concerned about oversleeping, we can try using an alarm clock that has a CD player or a radio that is set to soothing music to awaken us gradually and peacefully. Dolphin sounds are nice to wake up to.

5. Upon awakening, it is helpful for us to remain calm with closed eyes and in the reverie state (the level between wakefulness and sleep) for a few minutes as we recall our dreams. Gently shifting our physical position may also assist with recall. Dreams, like echoes, begin clearly but quickly fade after awakening. It is helpful to go to sleep earlier and awaken earlier than usual so we are not rushed.

6. Some herbs, such as passion flower, valerian and lavender may enhance sleep and relaxation. Mugwort may help us increase dream recall. The oracles of

Delphi used belladonna to induce dreams.[9] We can make dream pillows and stuff them with these sleep and dream inducing herbs.

7. There are also several essential oils which can help us relax and increase our dream recall. Lavender, bergamot, cedarwood, chamomile (Roman and German), mandarin, Melissa, Mugwort, orange, sandalwood, tangerine, tansy, valerian. There are also a few special oil blends by a company called Young Living that promote peace, sleep, and enhance dreams: Citrus Fresh, Dream Catcher, and Peace and Calming.

8. Certain stones and crystals can also help enhance sleep and dream recall. Crystals and gemstones work in different ways to help us with our dreams. Crystals work by amplifying the subtle energies that exist within a person. For example, if we feel very loving, and we have a crystal near our bed, it will enhance this loving energy while we sleep. A stone works by emitting an energy that focuses on one area only, such as happiness. Placing a stone or stones near our bed that vibrate(s) with the energy of intuition will help improve our dream recall. A pretty bowl with certain crystals and gemstones can be placed near our bed, and we can experiment with different ones to see what happens in our dreams! Gemstones to promote relaxation and enhanced dream recall include arfvedsonite, blue quartz, covelltie, crystal, dumortierite, orange elestial, howlite, lapis lazuli, merlinite, scolecite, and ulexite.

9. Daily meditation helps enhance dream recall because it opens up the door between the conscious mind and subconscious mind. Listening to our inner self/ subconscious mind in meditation is similar to listening

---

[9] *Retrieved from online. http://www.lucid-mind-com/facts-about-dreams.html.n.d.web20April,2014.*

to and watching our dreams. Dream symbols come from the subconscious mind just as messages in meditation can come from the subconscious mind.

10. Proper spinal alignment can help with dream recall because it helps us sleep better and ensures proper nerve function. When our spines are misaligned, we can experience problems which interfere with sleep, such as migraine headaches, fatigue, lower-back pain, arthritis, bedwetting, digestive disorders, nervous dysfunction, stiff neck, shoulder and arm pain, and insomnia. By correcting spinal misalignments, we can ensure better blood flow, increased circulation, increased delivery of oxygen, removal of lactic acid, and overall greater relaxation. Given the glands (pituitary and hypothalamus) and hormones (serotonin, melatonin) involved in the sleeping and dreaming process, it makes sense that general overall better health through correct spinal alignment can have a positive effect on hormones and glandular secretion. After completing a strenuous home relocation, my husband and I suffered from spinal misalignment. We noticed during this time that we were also having trouble remembering our dreams and our quality of sleep had deteriorated. Since we were in a new location, it took us a few weeks to locate a good chiropractor. After we had several adjustments, we noticed our sleep improved, as well as our dream recall.

CHAPTER 6:
DREAM SCENARIOS

What we experience in dreams—assuming that we experience it often—belongs in the end just as much to the overall economy of our soul as anything experienced "actually." We are richer or poorer on account of it.

—Friedrich Nietzsche, *Beyond Good and Evil*

Misunderstood dreams have been the source of worry for many people. Dreams of car crashes, illnesses and death have fed dreamers' fears that they might come true. Accurate interpretation may ease or even eliminate these worries. Although precognitive dreams may reveal future events, the majority of dreams do not reflect actual events.

The following dreams and their interpretations that may sound familiar are opportunities for us to try using these suggestions in our lives as guides to begin our own interpretations.

CHEERS!

This dreamer had a little too much wine at dinner.

Dream: *I am at a restaurant with my aunt and cousin. I am drinking wine, and my head is bandaged. I realize people are probably looking at me strangely because my head is bandaged.*

Interpretation: She is focusing on a part of herself that is disciplined (symbolized by the aunt, whom she describes as a very disciplined person) and a part of herself that is not disciplined (symbolized by the cousin). There is a problem with the dreamer's thinking process (symbolized by the bandaged head.)

Dreams like this are common after drinking a little too much because alcohol impairs the thinking processes and motor skills. Another symbol might be losing control of our car while driving since a car is symbolic of the physical body.

PREGNANT PAUSE

Learning the meaning of a recurring dream lifted a weight for this dreamer.

Dream: *A mother of nine, I have frequent dreams of being pregnant. My hands were full with children; the thought of having more sent me into depression. I was raised as a Catholic and do not use birth control. However, since these dreams began I decided to take extra precautions. I lie awake at night worrying how I would handle another child. Due to this dream, I lost interest in being intimate with my husband.*

Interpretation: Children represent new ideas. This dreamer had tons of ideas running through her mind but never had the time to develop them. This explained why she didn't dream of giving birth, which would represent ideas being realized. To end her frustration, a reflection of not being able to develop her ideas, she planned to spend 30 minutes a day focusing on developing one of her ideas.

TRUST YOURSELF

A clear understanding of recurring dreams of betrayal helped this dreamer pursue and fulfill her life's dreams.

Dream: *In recurring dreams, my partner was cheating on me. The dreams were accompanied by feelings of extreme anxiety. When this dream first began, I was considering attending an out-of-town school, which would require a year of seclusion. I was both excited and apprehensive about the program.*

Interpretation: This message has to do with not trusting her inner self (represented by her partner cheating on her). Once she entered the program, the dreams stopped.

A SNIPPET REVEALS IT ALL

Dream: I have had a recurring dream for years where I am searching for a bathroom and a toilet, and cannot find one. The dream brought up feelings of frustration and anxiety.

Interpretation: A bathroom in a dream symbolizes a place in mind where one can release unneeded thoughts and feelings. A toilet symbolizes a tool of the mind that helps one release old thoughts that are no longer useful to the self. This lady needs to release thoughts.

This lady shared with us that she was married to a man who didn't like to talk much. He worked long hours, and when he arrived home at night, he just wanted to sit and relax in peace and quiet. This lady didn't work outside the home, and so she wanted to share conversation when her husband got home, yet he was not receptive to that. In addition, she was a Libra Sun Sign, which is an air sign that enjoys socializing. The sign is also one that dislikes conflict and tends to hold things in that might rock the boat. This lady was a chain smoker, which has been linked to a form of emotional escape for people. We believe the repression of her thoughts led her to smoke. Basically she was mentally and emotionally constipated, backed up with thoughts she couldn't express.

DREAMS OF THE YOUNG, MIDDLE-AGED AND THE ELDERLY

Do certain age groups have a common dream thread? Our years of teaching have shown us that certain dreams are common to certain age groups, based on the thoughts that surround them.

CHILDREN AND NIGHTMARES

Children often experience nightmares. The big scary monster chasing them often represents their belief that something bigger than them is in charge of their lives. This could be any adult in their lives (parent/s, teachers, neighbors, etc.) and what is scary to them is that they are not allowed to make decisions for themselves. Our daughter's 5 year old friend from kindergarten, Jennifer, told us about a recurring nightmare that started after Jennifer's mother started dating a new man. Up to that point it had only been Jennifer and her mother living together, and her mom's new boyfriend was upsetting to her.

Dream: *A two-headed dragon is walking down the hallway in my house or is invading the city.*

Interpretation: She feels out of control in her life. She feels that there are things happening to her that are overwhelming, as is symbolized by the dragon.

Jennifer's mom attributed the dragon dreams to a movie called, "How to Train Your Dragon." We explained that the movie wasn't the cause of her dream. Her dream was caused by thoughts of not having control over her life, which were related to the new person in her mother's life. Jennifer's brain searched for the most recent symbol in her brain that related to being out of control, which was the dragon movie.

We recommend to her to allow Jennifer to make more choices for herself and engage her in activities that would help her feel powerful and in charge of her life. We also suggested she teach Jennifer more about dreams with the children's book *The Dream Doctor*.

TEEN DREAMS

Common teenage dreams revolve around issues of freedom, life purpose, discipline, conflict, creation and limitations. Teens are often faced with realizing the limitations and rules set by their parents, teachers, and society in general. Those teens who feel mentally limited by these outer factors will dream of being walled in, blocked by a fence, or find themselves in prison. Other teens may feel exhilarated by freedoms that come from receiving a driver license or being able to drink alcohol. Teens who feel the freedom of moving into adulthood and have high hopes for a bright future will have flying dreams, reflecting their belief that they can do and have anything they desire.

The increasing ability to create is also a key feature of teen dreams. Teens are experiencing more freedom in being able to create what they want in their lives. This ability to create their desires is mirrored by their body's ability to reproduce leading to images of sex showing up for the first time. Since people in a dream represent different parts of the dreamer, reproduction is the ability to change the self through learning and creation. A baby in a dream is a new idea or personality trait that has been birthed and is developing within the consciousness. An example of this may be the discovery of a love for music or a talent for writing. Sex in a dream for teens and adults represents a harmony that is occurring between the inner and outer selves that is stimulating the creative energies and has the potential to bring something new into the dreamer's life. When our conscious thoughts and actions are aligned with who we are inside, sex dreams may appear to show this alignment.

With the added freedoms that some teens experience, also comes the issue of discipline. Rebellious teens who defy authorities in their lives may have dreams of policemen to remind them of the need for discipline. This tumultuous time in life can also lead to inner conflict with different aspects within the self. For example, some teens may love to study but reject that part of themselves so that they won't look like nerds in school. As a result they might dream of fighting with people. For some teens, it is the first time in their lives when they begin to wonder about their life purpose. Their dreams might have hands as a predominant feature, which symbolize life purpose. Here is a dream from a 16-year-old girl.

Dream*: I am sitting in high school and looking at my hands. I notice I have pen marks all over my hands. I ask the teacher if I can go to the bathroom to wash my hands, and he says no. I am mad at him and leave the room to go to the bathroom when he is not looking. In the hallway I am stopped by a hall monitor who asks to see my room pass. I don't have one, so he gives me a detention.*

Interpretation: This girl is focused on learning about her life purpose (hands). There is something about her life purpose that draws her attention, and she wants to be able to be able to release those things distracting her from her purpose (pen marks). However, the part of her that is focused on learning (teacher) is not in alignment with her desire. She feels that she needs to avoid and ignore this part of herself to get what she wants. A disciplined part of herself (hall monitor) catches this moment of rebellion within her thinking and moves her to take a moment of self-reflection (detention).

MIDDLE-AGED ADULTS

FEMALE

In our classes we help students identify themes in their dreams. One of our students, a middle-aged woman and mother of two boys, with a full-time medical practice, had recurring dreams that reflected her need for rest and relaxation. In one class she stated that she would love to go to Tibet for a year and meditate. Clearly, her hectic lifestyle was not allowing her time to practice spiritual disciplines and was beginning to wear on her. Below are two examples of a common dream for middle-aged working mothers:

Dream: *I am relaxing and enjoying my life. My son Tom and someone else's child are with me, having a good time. I look up at the sky, and it is a night sky with beautiful stars even though it is daytime. I want to study the stars and tell the kids to go out to the shore with me. I want to lie down in a chair to look at the stars. Just as I lay down Tom informs me that the kid with us is missing. I glance at the sky. The stars are so bright I can see constellations but have to look for the kid. We find her. I tell her she must always stay close. I try to lay down again so I can study the sky. Now Tom tells me that another girl lying next to us, but not with us, has been teasing our girl and took her toy away. I go to her and tell her to give the toy back. Before I can lie down again to look at the sky, I look at the sea. There are big waves far out in the sea coming our way. I sense danger and tell my kids it's time to go. At the hotel lobby I look at the sea. The water is receding into the sea and I know a tsunami is coming. We are running away, and I am searching for a plan. The wave comes in, and I'm gasping for air but not scared.*

Interpretation: This person is enjoying life and is connecting with her superconscious mind where she gains greater awareness; however, she keeps getting distracted by new ideas (the children). She tries to return to the peace of her superconscious mind; however, this time she gets distracted by feelings of being emotionally overwhelmed (running away) by her life. Though she tries, she can't escape her emotions and eventually they get the best of her (gasping for air in the water).

Here is a slightly different dream, with a similar message.

Dream: *It is late in the evening, and I am at the computer, looking out the window. I see an empty school bus driving by. It feels out of place. Suddenly the bus pulls into my open garage. I tell my son Tom to lock the garage door. I go outside* *the front door to confront the driver. I ask the driver what he is doing parking in my garage. He says he needed a place to park the bus. This makes no sense to me as there is plenty of room on the street. The bus driver drives away and then parks in my neighbor's garage. I call 911 and request for the police to come deal with this crazy bus driver.*

Interpretation: The dreamer recognizes it is time to assimilate her daily experiences (evening time) by reviewing her mind and brain (computer) to gain a greater awareness. However, part of her mind is still focused on getting to a place of learning (the school bus). She knows it is not time to think about learning (feeling that it is out of place and time.) The part of her that gets her to a place of learning (bus) is invading her place for physical rest and rejuvenation (garage). She is out of harmony with the part of herself that helps her get to places of learning (the bus driver) and is reaching out to other parts of herself to deal with this part of herself (symbolized by calling 911).

MALE

The pressures of middle-aged men to get ahead in the world are reflected in their dreams. A man we know was climbing the corporate ladder at Kinko's. He had already gone from store manager of two different locations to being a district manager for 26 stores.

Dream: *He had recurring dreams of showing up late for school in his pajamas and not being able to find his classroom.*

Interpretation: This dream symbolizes his insecurities about being prepared for life. He felt pressure to perform more at work, and this pressure to constantly perform better usually left him feeling unprepared for the task. He was losing interest in the day-to-day tasks after 15 years on the job. The school represents a place within him where he is focused on learning. Showing up unprepared and being unable to find the right room shows that he isn't really learning new things in his life, yet he is yearning to grow and learn.

This man eventually left this career and pursued his passion of restoring and selling antique furniture. As a result of doing what he loves, these dreams have stopped.

ELDERLY

Many elderly people often focus on the past when they have nothing to look forward to in the future. It is common for them to dream of cemeteries, which represent the past. You might hear elderly people talk about how they used to be creative and funny or a great dancer. These are the parts of themselves they have buried in the cemetery. We have also had many elderly folks describe dreams with snow and ice. Snow and ice are frozen water, which signifies unchanging and stagnant life experiences due to emotional stagnation. When someone becomes sedentary and does the same thing every day and becomes stuck in an emotional rut, his/her life is like ice, where there is no flow or movement.

SEXY AND SIZZLING

Dream: *I was finally alone with Steve. He began rubbing my back and shoulders and slowly moved to massage my entire body. Then I felt his lips touch my back, and so I turned to face him and ...bzzzzzzz.*

Darn! The alarm clock went off.

Does this sound familiar? We all want these dreams to continue because being intimate with someone we love feels good, just as it does in waking life. So, what can we do to make this dream recur? The dream reflects a person who has a harmonious relationship with her inner self or subconscious mind. In order to create anything in life, we need the cooperation between our conscious and subconscious minds. The conscious mind forms desires and the subconscious aids in fulfilling them. To recreate a sex dream, we need to continue to deepen our relationship with the inner self.

Suppose we have a desire to buy a new car. We think about the color, model, and price we want to pay. We search the internet and tell our friends what we are looking for. Meanwhile our subconscious mind is hard at work attracting the right car for us. Suddenly a cousin calls who is selling a car exactly like we imagined. We go, look at the car, and purchase it. This is an example of harmony when everything flows and our desires are fulfilled. To understand what aspects of ourselves are in harmony, we need to identify the qualities that the people represent in our waking life.

No need to worry if we find ourselves having sexual encounters with people other than our partner since it only reflects we are harmonizing with an aspect of ourselves. What about sex with the same sex? Again, this does not reflect someone's sexual preference; rather, it reflects how they are using the mind to create. Procreation requires both a male and female to succeed. In a similar way creating with our mind requires both the masculine aggressive energy and the feminine receptive energy to succeed. Therefore, in a dream where we are having sex with someone of the same gender, we are experiencing pleasure and harmony, but without the potential to create something new in our life. This is similar to masturbation.

In dreams, a person of the opposite sex represents how we view our masculine or feminine selves. Having sex with a person of the same gender indicates we are creating with only one aspect of self (either the feminine or masculine energy). Creating this way can be difficult since we are only using part of our mind. If we are male and only having sex with males, it's time to notice if we are rejecting our intuition, the messages from the inner self, which are part of the feminine energy. If we are female and dream only of having sex with females, it's time for us to notice if we are afraid to use our aggressive energy in our creations. This would be evident if we get ideas and develop them in our mind but never take any physical steps to get our ideas out into the world. When we create using both the masculine and feminine energy, it becomes easier.

Dream: *"I'm sorry, Steve, but I can't have sex with you because I don't have any birth control," Susan tells him in the dream. Steve replies, "You have been pursuing me for months now and teasing me with sexual innuendos. I don't like a tease." Steve proceeds to rape Susan.*

Interpretation: In this case Susan is afraid that her creations may actually come to fruition. Have you ever wanted something, yet were afraid of what would happen if you got it? This reflects how she was rejecting something in her life that she asked for. Susan is fighting the manifestation of her own desires. Steve represents an aspect of her subconscious mind, which is simply doing its duty by creating what she has desired in her conscious mind. Our subconscious mind does not force things on us. Sometimes, however, we may feel as though our inner self or life is forcing something to happen to us. In these experiences we are helped by remembering that our life is only a reflection of what we have been focusing on in our thoughts.

OOPS, I'M PREGNANT.

Pregnancy in a dream indicates that a new idea or aspect of self is about to emerge. Remember that people are aspects of us, so a birth is something new emerging within us. This can be a love of music, a gift for sports, or a newly developed sense of generosity. The possibilities are endless. If the dreamer realizes she is pregnant and decides to have an abortion, this symbolizes the rejection of a new idea. In her waking life the dreamer has formed some ideas about what she wants but then rejected them.

BREAKING UP

Even in a dream, breaking up is hard to do. When we divorce or break up with a partner, this means we have broken a commitment with our inner self. To understand this better, let us look at the commitment that has been made to the other person in the dream. Being married in a dream is much more significant than living together, for example. This reflects the commitments that we make in our waking life, only these commitments are with ourselves. If we are honest about the qualities of the other person in the dream, we will see the nature of the commitment that we have made.

MARRIAGE

In a dream, marriage signifies we are making a commitment to our inner self. Many girls dream of a knight in shining armor who comes to marry them, and together they live happily ever after. What we all long for is the connection with our inner self, which is why a marriage dream feels good. The main purpose of dream interpretation is to forge a deeper connection with our inner self. When we are ready to begin, we can read the tips for enhancing dream recall. We can then follow these steps and use the dream symbol guide to find the meaning of our symbols.

DREAMS OF SPIRITUALLY FOCUSED DREAMERS

People focused on spiritual growth will have dreams centered on symbols that are of a spiritual or religious nature, such as a cross, pentagram, or the Star of David. The people in the dreams tend to be spiritual leaders, such as priests or shamans, and our parents who represent our higher self. Typical places include churches or spiritual centers. Feet in a dream represent our spiritual foundation and frequently appear in dreams of those seeking spiritual enlightenment. Below is a dream from a woman who has been practicing spiritual disciplines for many years.

Dream: *I am sitting at a gate in an airport. I approach three women who are there, offer to take their shoes while they wait and say, "I would normally do reflexology for you, but there's not time...but you can give me your shoes." They are confused, wondering why they'd give me shoes without receiving reflexology. I say it will be nice to wait for the plane without shoes, but I realize even as I am saying this how silly it sounds. I take the three pairs of shoes with me to the bathroom and place them in cubbies that are outside of the bathroom. The interior of the bathroom is a larger version of an airplane bathroom—very different. When I come out, I try to pick up the shoes, but now the cubbies are overloaded with other people's shoes, and I don't remember what their shoes look like. I only remember one pair—green flip-flops.*

I am nervous because I think we will all miss our flight. Next I am walking back to the gate (don't know what happened with the shoes), and my mom is there, needing me to get her something before the flight takes off. I am angry at her. Why did she wait? And I want her to get what she needs on her own.

Interpretation: She is looking at how she expresses her spirituality in different groups and by herself. The airport represents a place where her mind is blending with the minds of many others. Commercial jets represent organizations in her life and the many possibilities that exist for her. She is more focused on the outer way she expresses her spirituality rather than actually wanting to do something to create a stronger spiritual foundation (focusing on the shoes rather than doing reflexology on the feet, which would nourish them and the whole body). Part of her is confused about her emphasis on giving attention to the outer expression rather than the inner. Her focus on the outer expression of her spirituality and the desire to be totally open, and exposing her beliefs seems silly to her (taking off the shoes to wait for the plane). She feels the need to let go of those thoughts (going to the bathroom), and after she does, she recognizes there are so many ways to express her spirituality that she has trouble distinguishing which ways are truly her ways and not someone else's (all of the shoes outside the bathroom door). She has anxiety because she feels she has not learned enough and is not where she should be spiritually (fearing she will miss the flight). This type of thinking puts her in conflict with her higher self that she feels is demanding and asking too much of her (being angry at her mother for making a request).

CHAPTER 7:
SHAPING YOUR DREAMS

Last night I dreamed I ate a ten-pound marshmallow, and when I woke up the pillow was gone.

—Tommy Cooper

If we want to create pleasurable dreams, there are several things we can do to attain this. Since dreams are a reflection of our thoughts and attitudes, we can focus on positive, productive thoughts throughout our day. We can also love and praise ourselves and cooperate with our inner desires; if we want something, we must take steps to manifest it. Fighting in a dream occurs when we are not cooperating or liking parts of ourselves. We must be nice to ourselves, and if we find there are parts of ourselves we dislike, we must find ways to change them or make them useful. For example, if we dislike our tendency to be impatient, we acknowledge that part of us and validate it for helping us get things done. When it becomes a nuisance, we then tell it that we will eventually do what it wants us to do, but now is not the right time. These actions will also help you achieve intimate and sexy dreams. If we are affectionate and kind to ourselves throughout the day, we will be rewarded at night with that same behavior projected toward us by the people in our dreams. If there is a particular person we want to be intimate with in the dream, we can think about the most outstanding qualities of that person and develop those qualities in ourselves. The more we become like that person, and express those qualities, the more likely it is that person will appear in our dream.

We can influence the dream state with our intentions. One of the great benefits of dreams is the ability to receive answers to problems or questions. Before bed we can state the guidance we desire on a particular problem. Our subconscious can then give us the answers in our sleep. It is easier for the subconscious to communicate to us when our conscious mind is asleep and quiet, which is why many people receive insights to problems while sleeping.

There was a dream experiment that was announced in the April 10, 2012, issue of "Science Daily." In it the researchers used music to influence people's dreams while they slept. The music, which they called the "soundscape," was created to induce a pleasant dream scenario. A song can trigger a memory or evoke a certain emotion. Since dreams reflect thoughts and attitudes during the day, it could be more beneficial to have the person listen to the "soundscape" or peaceful music during the day, allowing the music to foster pleasant thoughts. While the notion of influencing dreams through the music that we listen to while we sleep is intriguing, we propose that the purpose of dreams is to develop a deeper understanding of ourselves. Using music to manufacture a certain kind of dream defeats this purpose. If we use music during the day to enhance our peace and mental clarity, it can affect our dream state indirectly by affecting our thoughts. The most effective way to influence our dreams is to change our thoughts.

Music can slow a person's breathing and heartbeat and put them into deep relaxation. Music can relieve pain by causing the body to release endorphins that reduce pain. Music has been used in educational settings because of its ability to improve concentration, attention, memory, and intelligence. When we do something that affects our brain and thinking, we can see a change in our dreams since dreams reflect our thinking. Check out Steven Halpern's music or Don Campbell's book *The Mozart Effect: Tapping the Power of Music to Heal the Body, Strengthen the Mind, and Unlock the Creative Spirit* to learn more how music can affect our mind.

Spiritual practices can have a profound effect on dream content and recall. The reason is that the goal of most spiritual disciplines is to get us more in touch with our subconscious mind, which is where dreams originate. If we consciously bring more awareness to our subconscious mind, then when we go to sleep at night, it will be easier for us to be aware in the dream state. Any type of practice devoted to spiritual enlightenment will result in dream symbols, such as churches, priests, and grandparents (aspects of the superconscious mind).

Many spiritual practices, such as meditation, can bring greater peace and quiet to the mind. A quiet mind is more receptive to messages from the subconscious mind. The more we practice meditation, the more familiar we become with the way the subconscious communicates.

Yoga, which means union, is practiced to unite the conscious, subconscious and superconscious minds, as well as the mind and body. This is beneficial to remember and interpret our dreams. Yoga also relieves mental and physical tension, which creates a more peaceful sleep and better dream recall.

Our religion will also affect dream content and recall. If our religion believes in the importance of dreams, we are more likely to remember them since we have the thought that they are important. The dream content will be influenced by our thoughts, which are shaped by many things, including our religion. For example, if we practice a "new thought" spiritual path that says we are powerful, limitless creators, then we may have dreams of flying (indicating we are free thinkers who do not limit ourselves). If we practice Buddhism, we may have harmonious dreams of dancing since that religion teaches kindness to self and others.

CHAPTER 8:
DREAM SYMBOL GLOSSARY

Trust in dreams, for in them is hidden the gate to eternity.

—Kahlil Gibran, *The Prophet*

Dream interpretation is the art of understanding the symbolism of the people, places and things in dreams and then applying the dream's message to your life. If you review your dreams every month or so, you will begin to notice which items, actions and tones recur to discover themes. As you make changes in your life based on your dream awareness, you will notice a change in your dreams.

As you apply the information in the glossary, remember to keep in mind the following:

- *Aspect of self* refers to a quality, characteristic or personality trait of the dreamer.
- *Habit* refers to a physical habit, such as nail biting or a mental habit, such as worrying.
- *Mental tool* refers to a way of thinking (e.g., imagination, focus, concentration, or reasoning) that helps the dreamer perform a task or create something.
- *State of mind* refers to how you are feeling.

Abortion: An idea was about to be birthed into the life, but then you stopped the visualization necessary to bring the idea to fruition. Ask why you stopped nurturing your idea. If you were uncertain whether or not you could handle the new idea in your life, it would be beneficial to practice spiritual disciplines and ask for help. If you think of an idea, you are capable of executing it.

Actor: An actor reveals using your imagination to play different roles in your life. This can be productive, such as imagining what it is like to have money if you are in need of greater prosperity, or it can be counterproductive, such as hiding your true self by pretending to be someone else. If the latter is the case, ask why you do not show your real self and realize that the true you is the most interesting person in the world.

Adult: A mature, experienced aspect of yourself.

Adventure: You are curious and open to new things, which allows you to embrace new learning.

Ahiṃsā Hand: See *Religious Symbol*.

AIDS (Acquired Immune Deficiency Syndrome): You are focusing so much attention on defending your identity that it becomes destructive. You would benefit from practicing self-love, self-acceptance, forgiveness and release.

Air: How your thoughts are moving through your mind. Fast wind indicates you are thinking quickly. If you are having difficulty breathing, this signifies a difficulty formulating or processing thoughts.

Airplane: This symbol shows how you are using your thoughts to move forward in life to accomplish something. If there are many people on the plane, it shows you are uniting your thoughts with others of like mind to accomplish a goal; such as in an organization. Since an airplane travels fast, it shows you are using your mind to obtain a goal in a quick fashion.

Airport: A place in your mind where you may connect with other minds. This is sometimes referred to as *Universal Mind* because it is where all of our minds connect and communicate with each other. This is also where you unite with people of like mind to accomplish a goal or mission. An organization (symbolized by an airplane), helps us accomplish things that we could not do alone, which is why we often refer to an organization as a vehicle like an airplane.

Alcohol: Drinking alcohol indicates that you are doing something in your life that is weakening your willpower. Your willpower allows you to use your mind effectively. You weaken your willpower every time you have an opportunity to make progress toward a goal you have set for yourself but instead procrastinate or become distracted by unimportant things.

Alien: An aspect of yourself that is completely unfamiliar to you. It is a part of yourself that may seem bizarre and engender fear.

Amusement Park: A state of mind focused on having fun. Nothing is being created other than a pleasant state of mind. However, this can be valuable if, for example, you have been depressed or stressed.

Animals: Habits. Positive habits, such as brushing your teeth are helpful; whereas negative habits, such as worrying can hinder your growth. The size and nature of the animal reveals the type of habit. A pet or other harmless creature indicates a small habit, such as nail biting. An alligator that is attacking you represents a habit that can cause harm in your life, such as smoking. If you are feeding the animal, you did something that day to encourage the habit. If the animal is viciously pursuing you, you feel that the habit controls you.

Antiques: Tools within yourself that have value because you have used them over a long period of time.

Army: Many aspects of yourself that are working together to cause change or prevent it. If the army is attacking another force, identify who it is attacking to understand the parts of you that you want to change. If the army is defending against an invader, look at your life to see if you are resisting change. If the change that you are resisting is productive, realize the energy used to hold back change can be used for other productive purposes.

Art: Creativity. You are exercising your imagination to create something. You may also be using other mental skills (such as reasoning) in the process of creation.

Artillery: Tools for causing change. Artillery is capable of changing things very quickly. This is often very destructive. You may be tearing something down in your life to replace it with something new.

Ashram: A place in mind for quiet reflection and focusing on your inner self.

Authority Figures (grandparents, parents, teachers, policemen, etc.): Your higher self or superconscious mind. Authority figures offer guidance and keep us centered in our life purpose, just as our higher self does. Interactions with authority figures reveal you have been consulting your higher self. The type of interaction you have with these people indicates your relationship to your higher self.

Autumn: See *Seasons*.

Award: Represents the recognition of an accomplishment or proficiency in an area of your life. The type of award will reveal the nature of the accomplishment or proficiency. A singing award, for example, indicates that the dreamer has learned to create harmony in the life effectively.

Ballet: Harmony that is created with much discipline and effort.

Bank: Money in a dream symbolizes self-value, so a bank means you recognize great value within yourself. A bank may be a place in your life where you recognize your value.

Banquet: Symbolizes your awareness that there is a variety of knowledge available.

Basement: The unconscious part of your mind. This is an area of your mind you don't often visit that contains many parts of yourself of which you are not consciously aware. It benefits you to become aware of this because many things in the unconscious will still affect your life. Awareness is the first step to creating positive changes.

Bathing: The practice of "cleaning up" your thoughts and attitudes and removing emotional garbage that is affecting your self-expression in a negative way. If we look dirty and are stinky, it is difficult to portray a positive self-expression.

Bathroom (going to the): You are letting go of experiences and knowledge that are no longer needed.

Bathroom (place): A place in your life where you are focusing attention on releasing memories, feelings, and thoughts that are no longer productive for yourself.

Battle: Inner conflict. The people who are fighting represent the parts of yourself that are in conflict. You will benefit by creating a clear goal so that you can coordinate your efforts to fulfill the goal.

Beach: A beach is typically a serene place. You can easily observe and connect with your emotions without having to get immersed in them. If you dream of a day at the beach, it means that you were existing in a state of mind where you were enjoying your daily experiences while maintaining a connection to a deeper part of yourself.

Bed: Tool to help you relax your mind and assimilate your experiences from the day. This tool could be the ability to still your mind to create deep, peaceful brainwave activity.

Bedroom: A place in mind for assimilation of your daily experiences and relaxation.

Bells: Tools of the mind for getting your attention. The type of bell reveals what you need to focus on. A school bell means you need to focus on learning, and a church bell signifies you need to pay attention to your spirituality.

Bible: A holy work symbolizes spiritual knowledge. This knowledge is called the "Universal Laws and Truths."

Bill: You have received something of value. If it is a restaurant bill, you have received knowledge that has value. It would benefit you to practice gratitude for all the things you have received in your life.

Bird: Habitual ways that you create a sense of freedom in your mind. These habits can be quite productive since they allow you to move beyond boundaries and limitations in your thinking. Examples may include doing a daily meditation or using positive affirmations.

Birth: The act of giving birth signals you have created a new idea or way of thinking. Celebrate this and nurture the new idea to adulthood.

Birthday: A birthday marks the completion of a cycle. You have spiritually or mentally matured, and this is cause for a celebration. Notice what you have been doing in your life to cause this growth and continue these efforts.

Blindness: You were having difficulty with perception. You may be having trouble looking at a part of yourself. You would benefit from meditation.

Blizzard: Conflict and turmoil in your mind due to a resistance to change. Examine why you are refusing to change, and then look at the possible benefits of making a change.

Blood: Blood is what physically keeps your body alive and life force or cosmic energy is the energetic counterpart to the blood. If you have a dream of bleeding, it means that something in your life is depleting your life force. You would benefit from focusing on your life purpose and doing spiritual exercises to increase the flow of your life force energy, such as Tai Chi.

Boat: This indicates how you are using your emotions to move through life. Since water represents your emotions, the ease with which the boat is moving through the water indicates how well you have control over your emotions. If the boat sinks, it reveals the experiences are overwhelming you. If the boat is easily moving through the water, this indicates you are emotionally balanced and hence able to move through them with ease.

Body: Your body is the vehicle for your soul, and your thoughts influence the condition of your vehicle or body, so a body in a dream signifies your mental attitudes. A strong healthy body signifies positive and productive thoughts. A weak body signifies an indecisive wavering attitude or negative thoughts.

Bomb: Powerful tool within yourself that has the capability to change many of your ways thinking and self-aspects at once. Perhaps you have learned a new healing technique or are in the process of receiving counseling that is profoundly affecting your ability to change your life.

Book: Knowledge. Notice the type of book to know what type of knowledge you are examining.

Bookstore: A place in the mind where there is access to a wide variety of information. Unlike a library, you must purchase the books for a price. Therefore, you are recognizing the value of the information.

Bowl: A tool to help you contain and receive knowledge. Can you imagine eating soup on a plate? It would be just as difficult to learn something new when your mind is scattered and unfocused. You need the proper mental tools to learn, such as receptivity and focus.

Braces: A tool to improve the process of assimilating knowledge. You have become aware of a need to improve your mental skills, which could have been stimulated by the beginning of a new school year or entrance into college.

Brain: You were focused on understanding your thinking processes during the day. The brain is like a computer that stores information and performs various tasks. As you develop the power of your brain, you can increase your success and productivity. Practice concentration, visualization, and memory exercises.

Bridge: This signals you have made a significant transition in your life. When you cross a bridge, you have built a new neural pathway or type of thinking that has allowed you to open up to new ways of thinking.

Building: This reveals your state of mind. The type and condition of the building reveals the condition of your mind. A building that is well-built indicates a strong mind, whereas a building that is deteriorating indicates the mind is in need of attention. The type of building reveals where you are focusing your attention. For example, a church shows you are focusing on your spirituality.

Bus: A bus is an organization since it carries many people to a particular destination. The type of bus indicates what organization it serves. The bus is a tool for the organization to get its members in alignment with its goal. A school bus is a vehicle where the focus is on learning.

Cage: If you dream of being in a cage, you have become aware of limits and boundaries that exist in your mind that keep you "caged in." These are limited beliefs that you have formed about yourself and others.

Calendar: A tool to measure your learning and growth. In a dream, time passing indicates growth.

Camera: Memory. We take pictures of and remember what is important or beautiful to us. Notice what the camera is taking pictures of to know what is important to you at this time.

Campus (school): You are focused on learning.

Candy: Knowledge that is fun or satisfies the curiosity but does not add wisdom or help you in life. An example of candy knowledge would be reading a gossip magazine. Just as candy can eventually harm your teeth, reading too many gossip magazines can distort your perception of reality and take away precious time from other activities.

Car: The physical body. The condition of the car will reflect the condition of your body. A rusty, damaged car indicates your body is worn out and needs healing. The way the car is maneuvering through the street reveals how you are using your body to move through life. Each part of the car can be related to a specific body part. Brakes relate to your nervous system and the need to go faster or slow down. Hoses represent the various arteries and veins.

Carnival: You are focused on fun and enjoyment.

Cartoon: Since cartoon characters are imaginary, it reveals you are projecting a false image of yourself to the world or you are using your imagination.

Casino: State of mind where you want to gain value without much effort. The value may only be temporary, and you may feel worse if the gambling leads to a loss of money. This may also be taking risks in life that put your self-esteem in jeopardy. You need to find a permanent way of building lasting self-value, such as through positive affirmations and spiritual practices.

Castle: A place in mind that potentially has much value and where you see that you have a great deal of control over all parts of yourself.

Cat: A habitual pattern in your thinking and/or acting. An obvious trait of most cats is their love of sleep and relaxation. If you associate this with a cat, it reveals your habitual pattern of wanting to relax and zone out.

Cave: You have withdrawn your attention from the outer world in order to focus on your connection with your inner self. You will need to determine if you are avoiding something or desiring to attain a deeper connection within. Being in a cave can also represent delving into the unconscious parts of your mind.

***Cemetery*:** A place in mind where your attention is focused on the past and on aspects of yourself that are no longer a part of or relevant to you. If you dream of cemeteries, it would benefit you to focus on the present and formulate a list of desires so that you see you have a bright future.

***Chair*:** A chair is a mental tool that supports you and gives you stability, and also helps you relax your mind.

***Children*:** Aspects of yourself that you are in the beginning stages of developing. Enjoy this stage and nurture your dream children so they can mature into experienced and beneficial aspects.

***Choir*:** Harmony within the mind. You are using many aspects of yourself in a coordinated effort to create harmony.

***Christmas*:** Symbolizes the celebration and recognition of one's spiritual nature. It can also symbolize the beginnings of superconscious awareness within your consciousness.

Church (or other building of worship, such as a synagogue, temple, mosque, etc.): A state of mind focused on spirituality and your soul growth. If there are priests and other holy people present, you were connecting with various aspects of your superconscious mind.

***Circus*:** Your mind is focused on enjoyment of your talents that you do not commonly use in your daily life. If animals are involved, it indicates you are directing your habits. You are gaining control of the habits and are now able to direct them for your enjoyment.

***City*:** A state or condition of the mind. If you dream of a familiar city, you are engaged in thinking that is familiar to you. If you dream of an unknown city, you are thinking outside of your normal patterns. Identify your feelings and thoughts about the particular location to give you further clues about your state of mind. If you dream of a quiet beachside city, you are in a reflective, peaceful state of mind.

Cleaning tools: Mental tools to improve your thinking, such as concentration, memory, and imagination.

Cleaning: Represents the process of purifying your thoughts and eliminating that which keeps your mind unhealthy. This is a positive dream that indicates there has been a self-evaluation and you are taking steps to change your thinking that will pave the way for a better life.

Closet: A place in mind where you are aware of the different ways you express yourself. This may also be long term memory where you store tools of the mind you seldom use.

Clothes: The various ways you expresses yourself. If you are dressing differently in the dream than in your waking life, you are changing the way you express yourself to others. If you are purchasing new clothes, you are placing value on new ways of self-expression.

Cold (illness): You have been engaging in unproductive mental habits. This thinking usually indicates a type of indecision within you that causes you to sit on the fence rather than take action. You would benefit by examining your fear of taking action. Then replace your fear with positive affirmations, make the decision and take action!

Colors (Color/ Black and White): The color of the dream reveals on which level of mind, the dream is taking place. Black and white dreams take place in a level that is closest to the conscious level. This indicates you have not gone into a very deep sleep. Dreams in color indicate you are dreaming in deeper levels of mind and hence attaining a deeper sleep. The deepest levels are pastels and all white.

Computer: Symbolizes the brain. A computer processes information, which also is the function of the brain. The brain responds to your habits and thoughts. The brain pathways can be changed by you; you are the computer operator.

Conflict: Represents disharmony between various aspects of yourself. Identify who is fighting to determine what aspects are not in harmony. Suppose you identify the two people in the dream as creative and critical. You may notice in your waking life that every time you try to engage in a creative activity, you become critical of your creations and then give up.

Cooking: You are mentally preparing to receive new information.

Costume: Expressing yourself in a way that is fake and not your true self. This can also be using your imagination purposefully to imagine being different.

Country: Your current state of mind. If you are visiting a foreign country, you may be exploring new ways of thinking. The words you associate with the country describe the type of thinking and your state of mind.

Court: Your attention is on making a decision or resolving a conflict/challenge. You may call on many aspects of yourself to help in this process, represented by a judge and jury. It would benefit you to focus on the Universal Laws and in particular the Law of Cause and Effect.

Creator: Symbolizes the highest part of yourself. Whatever name you give to the Creator, such as God or Shiva, you have realized your natural ability to create anything you desire. Congratulate yourself for opening a door inside of yourself, which has given you access to amazing power and potential.

Credit Card: A way for you to access your value, even if you are not aware of it at the time. You can buy anything on credit even if you do not have the money to pay for it at the time. The things you are purchasing may bring you value so you can pay the credit card bill when it arrives.

Criminal: An aspect of yourself that does not see your innate value and thus your destroy yourself through dishonest actions. You would benefit by practicing self-love and positive thoughts.

Cross: See *Religious Symbol*.

Crowd or Audience: Many aspects of yourself that are gathered for a specific purpose. The type of gathering will reveal what you are focusing on. For example, a graduation will symbolize the recognition of an educational achievement or self-growth, and a party reveals your focus on fun.

Crown: A symbol of authority. If you are crowned the king or queen, your efforts have given you the ability to take charge of your life. You have gained authority over the many aspects of yourself and you recognize that you are in control of your mind and your life.

Cult: You have become so attached to a certain idea that it has taken control of your thinking processes. Your mind should be your servant, not your master. You would benefit from spiritual disciplines and visualization so you can regain control of your mind.

Dance: You are in alignment with your direction in life and the actions you are taking, which produces a feeling of harmony. When you are decisive instead of fighting with yourself about what direction to go, you move through life with grace and ease, just like a dancer.

Darkness: Lack of awareness. You feel confused and unclear about your purpose and actions.

Dawn: The light of the new day indicates a new understanding or awareness has just dawned on you. Light represents awareness.

Death: Change. If you dream that someone is killing you, you currently have the point of view that change is being forced upon you, and that you are not in control of the changes taking place in your life. The person killing you reveals the aspect that you feel is out of control and not acting in alignment with your whole self. If someone else is being killed, identify who is being killed to determine what part of yourself is being changed. If you are killing someone in a dream, it means that you are causing changes to take place in your life. Murder indicates forcing a change to occur while a natural death indicates a more natural change. Death is neither good nor bad. Identify if the change is desirable or not.

Death caused by disease represents that changes have occurred within you due to unproductive thinking. For example, hating yourself can lead to cancer. Death by old age reveals you have come to the end of a cycle and realize it is time to change. You have outgrown an old way of thinking. For example, most people naturally outgrow the egocentric childhood attitude that the world revolves around them. As we mature, many of the ways we thought as a child no longer serve us.

To determine what thoughts produce what physical imbalances, look at how the illness relates to a particular area of the body. For example, joints help us bend and flex, so mentally if we are rigid in our thinking, this will affect our joints and make them rigid or arthritic. Cancer eats away at the body just as thoughts of self-hatred eat away at our mind. Problems with the feminine reproductive system relate to difficulties using the feminine principle of receptivity while prostate problems relate to difficulties using the masculine principle of aggressiveness.

[In addition, anyone who is interested in exploring more about what specific thinking patterns cause what diseases can refer to the book *Heal Your Body* by Louise L. Hay.]

Desert: State or condition of mind where there is not much activity in terms of new ideas being cultivated or nurturing mature ideas. You are taking a mental vacation from thoughts, and must determine if this is related to avoidance and neglect or a physical condition that has impaired your ability to think, such as a stroke.

Devil: A part of yourself that is destructive and negative, such as an unproductive and out of control ego.

Diploma: You are recognizing an accomplishment. This would indicate an educational or personal growth achievement. Congratulate yourself!

Disease: Disease means you has been harboring negative thoughts for a long time that are now damaging your physical body. Negative thinking and fear destroy health and happiness. If you dream of disease, carefully examine and admit your fears, and then take steps to change your thinking through positive affirmations. The type of disease will indicate the types of negative thoughts you think. For further information, see **Death.**

Divorce: Symbolizes the breaking of a commitment to yourself. You are not harmonizing with your inner self, and the reason can be seen by looking at other clues in the dream. If infidelity is involved, you feel your inner self has betrayed you, perhaps because it has not manifested something you desire in life. If you are the one who cheated, you feel you have betrayed yourself in an overt way.

Doctor: An aspect of yourself that provides insight or guidance for you on how to use your mind productively to manifest your desires. This is a part of yourself that has understandings in health and healing.

Dog: A habitual pattern of your thoughts and/or actions. Dogs are known as man's best friend. The main characteristic they possess is their tendency to please their master. This habit can relate to the way you habitually try to please others in order to be liked and have friends.

Doll: A tool for developing the imagination. You are imagining the skills necessary to care for a developing part of yourself.

Door: A transition from one part of your mind to another. If it is locked you perceive a barrier to where you want to go.

Dragon: A habitual part of yourself that can be destructive. A dragon breathes fire which can cause rapid transformation.

Driving: You are exercising control over your body to move in a particular direction.

Drowning: Feeling overwhelmed by emotional life experiences. You would benefit from deep breathing exercises.

Drugs (drug abuse): If you dream that you are using or abusing drugs, it represents that you believe there are life experiences and mental states you crave that you cannot access and are beyond your control. You have given up your will-power. Many drugs, even some prescription drugs, weaken the will by impairing your ability to think and reason. Develop concentration and use visualization to build a strong mind.

Ears: Tools for listening (inner and outer). Your dream ears allow you to hear the inner self. Notice who or what you cannot hear in your dream. This is the part of yourself that you need to listen to. If you don't hear your mother in your dream, then you are most likely ignoring the messages from your higher self. Meditation is a way to develop inner listening skills. Inner listening often relates to outer listening as well.

Earth (soil): Subconscious Mind. Every idea that has come to fruition was first an idea in someone's mind. Just as there is a procedure for how plants grow, there is a mental procedure for how your ideas grow. If you dream of land that is filled with crops and flowers, then you have been cultivating many ideas. Planting seeds in a dream reveals you are taking the first step in the process of cultivating a new idea.

Earth (world): The whole mind. This includes the conscious, subconscious and superconscious mind. When you dream of the whole Earth, it reflects that your attention is on your life as a whole. This includes the spiritual, mental, emotional, and physical parts of your life.

Earthquake: There is a major transformation taking place in your life that is unexpected and scary because of the amount of change it can cause. There is tremendous release of energy associated with this change. It would benefit you to focus on the thoughts in your subconscious mind to create a strong spiritual foundation that is unshakable.

Election: You are deciding what aspects of yourself are best suited for certain tasks.

Elevator: A tool to help you move from one area or level of mind to another. Taking an elevator to the basement will take you to your unconscious mind, whereas taking it to the top floor will lead you into superconscious mind. Meditation is one example of a tool that can be used to do this.

Engagement: You are moving towards a full commitment towards an aspect of yourself.

Exercise: You are actively using your mind to perform various tasks. An acrobatic workout indicates you were using many advanced mental skills in a coordinated fashion. Exercises such as meditation and concentration will strengthen the mental muscle, which is your will power.

Eyes: Tools for perception. Blindness indicates you are not accurately perceiving what is happening in your life. If you dream of having perfect vision, you are indeed exercising your ability to perceive and notice what is happening around you.

Face: Generally we recognize and identify people by their faces. Since each person has a unique face, in a dream it symbolizes your own identity, and the many facets of you.

Factory: You are learning to be efficient and productive in your life. The items produced in the factory reveal in what area of life you wish to be more productive. A factory that produces cars reflects you are becoming more efficient in the way you use and develop your body.

Fall: See *Seasons*.

Falling: This symbolizes the movement of your attention from deep within your subconscious mind to your outer conscious mind. Many people are afraid to fall because they believe they will die in their waking life. Usually you will wake up when you hit the ground. If you hit the ground and die in your dream, it means your movement within the inner realms of your mind has caused you to change. The real reason you may fear falling in a dream is that it may change you!

Family Members: The aspects of yourself with whom you are most familiar and comfortable. You need to identify one or two qualities that describe the family member in your dream so you can understand what familiar quality you are dreaming about.

Farm: If the farm grows crops, you are using your mind to create knowledge. Growing plants can also represent the intentional use of visualization. If you use animals to help with the farming, such as a horse to pull a plow, then you are using habits to be efficient. Animal husbandry reveals you are habitual in your daily life.

Fear: This emotion sets the tone for the dream. You are misusing your imagination by focusing on what you don't want in life. Fear can be translated as "false expectations appearing real." It would benefit you to focus on what you do want in your life.

Feces: Knowledge that has already been used to its fullest and is no longer useful to you. This may be a signal that it is time to learn something new. If it is being used as fertilizer it indicates using past understandings to nourish new ones.

Feet: The condition of your feet in the dream reflects the spiritual foundation you stand on in your daily life. Foot problems reflect an unstable spiritual foundation that needs strengthening.

Fence: Boundary or self-imposed limitation. Since a fence is a structure erected to create a boundary or to define a space, a fence symbolizes a similar process within yourself. This can represent creating boundaries for your well-being or an imagined limitation that is preventing you from accomplishing a goal.

Fighting: Aspects that are in conflict.

Fire: Represents the process of transformation. You are expanding and transforming at a rapid rate. Look to see how fire appears to learn if you feel in control of this transformation or not. A house that is burning is different than a campfire. A house fire signifies expansion that you feel is out of control and destructive, while a campfire is more purposeful and in control.

Fish: Emotional habits. Since fish swim underwater, they represent habits that are deep within you, usually related to your emotions.

Flood: An overwhelming emotional experience or experiences that are challenging for you to process at once. You would benefit from meditation and concentration exercises to still your mind and assimilate life experiences so you do not feel so overwhelmed.

Flower: Recognizing the beauty of your subconscious mind. A flower is a plant that produces a beautiful and attractive bloom. Plants represent thoughts that are developing within your subconscious mind.

Flying: Symbolizes freedom in thinking where you do not entertain thoughts of limitation and defeat. This kind of dream reflects that you are an expansive thinker that likes to explore new ideas and possibilities.

Food: Knowledge. Food nourishes your body. Knowledge nourishes your mind. Identify if you are eating foods that are healthy for you or if you are eating junk foods that have no nutritional value. Food that is not eaten is information. It becomes knowledge when you make it a part of yourself.

Food (spoiled): Wasted knowledge. You have not used what you know, and so the knowledge has gone to waste. Spoiled food indicates the knowledge is no longer useful to you. Ask yourself why you allowed the knowledge to go to waste, and next time"use it or lose it."

Foreign Country: An unfamiliar place in your mind. Identify the thought you associate with this country to know what type of thinking you want to explore.

Forest: Subconscious Mind. This represents a fertile state of mind. If it is a strong, healthy forest, it reflects a strong state of mind where ideas easily form and take shape. If your dream forest is bare or has been destroyed, you see your inner mind as lacking life and vitality. In this latter case you may feel that it is difficult for you to manifest your desires.

Fountain: You are recognizing the beauty of your emotional life experiences.

Friends: Familiar aspects of yourself that you enjoy and are comfortable with. Use one or two words to describe each friend to identify the aspect.

Fruit: Beneficial knowledge. Since fruit digests easily, this is knowledge you can apply in your life easily.

Fuel: Valuable substance that sustains and provides energy to whatever you put it in. If you are putting fuel in a car, you are sustaining your body. This may be food and/or life force energy. For an organization this may be time or effort. If you fuel a train, this will sustain an organization.

Furniture: Tools of the mind to aid you to make your life easier. Imagine how difficult your life would be if you didn't have memory or imagination? Likewise your life would be very difficult without chairs, tables, or beds.

Game: Represents a state of mind where you see life as a game or competition. You may be using strategic thinking in your life or may be focused on winning.

Garage: A place to rest your body, which is symbolized by a car. If you dream of a garage, it signifies you are resting or need to rest your body.

Gas Station: State of mind where you see the need to take care of and re-energize your physical body. This may be a sign that you are skipping meals or eating foods that are not nutritious.

Gasoline: Energy level within the physical body. When you dream of being out of gas this means you need to pay attention to the energy you expend and may need refueling with nutrient dense food or life force building exercises like Tai Chi and Qigong. Concentration exercises will help you focus better throughout the day and make better use of your energy reserves.

Genitalia: Tools for creation. You can produce a baby with genitalia; therefore, it reflects your tools to create in your life. When you create a baby you are creating a new part of yourself.

Ghost: Your astral body. A ghost is the form a soul uses when moving about on the astral plane. You are aware that you can exist on levels other than the physical plane. A ghost may also represent a visit from someone who has passed on. If there is fear associated with the dream, you would benefit from meditation, and prayer. Release any negative or fearful thoughts surrounding ghosts and know that your positive energy will not attract evil spirits.

Giant: Aspect of yourself that is powerful, special, or being exaggerated in some way. You may be expressing yourself in a way to get attention from others. The self-expression may be ego-centered as well. The type of giant, friendly or evil, will give you more clues about this part of yourself.

Gift: You are recognizing something of value within yourself. The person who is giving or receiving the gift will give you further information about what you are recognizing of value within yourself. Open the gift to learn more about your value. For example, if you receive a CD of your favorite music, you have discovered how to create harmony.

Glasses: A tool within yourself to correct and enhance your perception. If you dream of wearing glasses, this could reflect your realization that you misperceived something and need to look closer. If you have blurred vision in a dream, ask yourself what you cannot or do not want to see. Meditation upon the third eye (the point between and slightly above the eyebrows) will help you enhance perception.

Gold: Value. Ask yourself, "What is precious and valuable within me?" Next to diamonds, gold is often considered one of the most precious substances. Gold can also represent inner wisdom because of its special properties and value.

Graduation: Represents the completion of a cycle of learning. You have learned something of value, which will prepare you for greater things to come. Celebrate your newfound awareness.

Grass: Subconscious thoughts that serve as the foundation for other ideas and thoughts.

Grocery Store: Place in mind where there is a variety of knowledge available to choose from. The food has a price, which means you need to value it in order to receive the knowledge. Notice the type of food you are choosing and its value to you.

Gun: A tool for causing change because death is change. A gun can also be used for enforcing control.

Hair: Represents your conscious thoughts and how you express them. If you dream of cutting your hair, you are in the process of releasing or changing your thoughts. A new hairstyle indicates a new way of expressing your thoughts. If you dream of someone who is bald, it means you are going through a transformation, and you have not yet formulated the thoughts that reflect the new you. If the dream person who is bald is an emotional person, then you are having difficulty expressing your emotions.

Hands: Hands reveal what you are doing with your life purpose. A broken hand symbolizes difficulty in fulfilling your life purpose.

Hat: You are hiding or concealing your thoughts. It takes energy to hold your thoughts in, so it would benefit you to express what is on your mind so you can have more energy to create with your thoughts. Also, a hat can be used as a form of self-expression like clothing. This would be related to your thoughts and identity. A hat can also be used for protection.

Head: You are gaining a deeper awareness of how you think. If your head is injured, you need to release the negative thinking that is causing the problem. The head and face together relate to your identity and how you think about this.

Healing modalities (such as acupuncture, herbs, Reiki): You are directing your thoughts to cause healing. You recognize the need for a holistic approach since you are aware of your mind/body connection and the energetic nature of your being.

Healing: You are changing your negative thoughts to more positive, higher vibrational thoughts to produce health and happiness. Since all disease begins in the mind, all healing must first start with attention to the thought process.

***Heart*:** You are focusing on your emotions and what is truly important for you at this time. It signifies where your "heart" is focused, perhaps on career, family, or learning. Heart can also be related to your inner understandings.

***Heaven*:** You are experiencing a spiritual, enlightened state of being. During the previous day you may have given and received love freely and without attachment.

***Highway*:** Path in life. This is the path or direction you are moving towards. This usually indicates a long-term goal that may take a while to manifest.

***Home*:** The mind. Also, a familiar state of mind. Home is where we physically live. The mind is where our consciousness lives.

***Horse*:** Represents willpower. Your will is helpful to you, just like a horse, and will get you to your desired destination. If you are having trouble getting your horse to cooperate, you need to build up your willpower through daily exercises and spiritual practices. When you ride a horse, you need to have a calm mind and a clear intention. These are the same qualities that you need when you activate your will to create your desires.

***Hotel*:** State of mind where you are connected to many other qualities of yourself and ways of experiencing life. Since anyone can go to a hotel, it also is a place in the subconscious mind (called the "universal mind") where we are all connected. Dreaming of a hotel signifies you were connecting with other people on a mental level.

***House*:** The mind. The condition of the house reflects your attitude about your mind. If you dream of a beautiful house in good condition, you see the value in your mind. A shack or house in disrepair indicates low self-esteem. Each room in a house indicates a different type of thinking. A bathroom is a place in mind for releasing your unwanted thoughts, and a bedroom is a place for assimilating your experiences (processing learning). The kitchen is where you prepare to receive knowledge, and you receive it in the dining room. The living room is a general purpose room where you spend most of your time.

Ice: Ice symbolizes that your emotional life experiences (frozen water) are stagnant and unchanging. It would benefit you to realize the nature of the physical is change, and resisting change can limit your spiritual growth. You need to identify why and what emotions you are afraid to change in your life and then move beyond those fears.

Insect: Insects, like animals, represent habits. Most harmless insects are small pesky habits that can be aggravating, like a mosquito. Think about the small aggravating habits you have that do not have a huge impact on your life but cause small interferences.

Insurance: You feel the need to protect yourself from something you fear could be harmful.

Internet: The universal mind, where you are able to connect with other people and have access to large amounts of information.

Invention: Through creative efforts you have produced something that will create greater efficiency and productivity within yourself.

Invitation: You have received some form of communication that can be an opportunity for growth. A birthday party invitation signals the opportunity to celebrate the end of one cycle and the beginning of a new one.

Island: You have isolated yourself and created a barrier to connecting with other aspects of yourself and other people. The isolation may be physical, emotional or mental. It would benefit you to share your thoughts with others to learn and grow and expand your thinking.

Jail: See *Prison*.

Jewelry: Value. Wearing jewelry represents that you are expressing how valuable you are to others. The degree of value is determined by the beauty and rarity of the stones and metals used in the jewelry.

Judge: Aspect of yourself that knows the Universal Laws and decides what is productive and unproductive. This is often referred to as your conscience. You can rely on this part of yourself to guide you through challenges. This aspect of yourself works with karmic lessons and cause and effect.

Jury: Aspects that weigh what is productive and unproductive and make a decision about the future. You have gathered various aspects of yourself to determine if something is in alignment with your purpose or not.

Key: Symbolizes your ability to access new parts of your mind and explore different ways of thinking and being. If you are using a key to unlock a door, it means that you are unlocking a new potential within your mind.

Killing: Death in a dream represents change. If you are killing, it means that you are consciously causing change. If you dream that you are being killed, it means that there is change going on, but from your perspective it is happening to you, and you are not in control of these changes in your life.

King: Aspect of yourself that is in charge and exercises control over many other aspects of yourself. In order to become king, you must prove yourself worthy. Likewise, in order to gain dominion over other aspects of yourself, you must prove worthy through effort and discipline. If this aspect goes unchecked, it can turn into an egotistical and dominating part of yourself.

Kiss: You are showing appreciation for an aspect of yourself. The person you are kissing is an aspect of yourself that you are harmonizing with and wanting to be close to.

Kitchen: Place in your mind where you prepare to receive knowledge. Cooking and eating can be an enjoyable activity that engages all of the senses, just as learning can be enjoyable and beneficial.

Knife: A tool to promote and cause change. Knives have many purposes that assist in the process of change. A chef using a knife in a dream to prepare food indicates you are preparing knowledge. A surgeon using a knife in surgery reveals you are healing part of your mind. If you or someone else is using a knife to kill someone, you/the person that represents you are causing permanent change (death) within yourself.

Labor (work): You are being productive. The type of work signifies in what way you are using your skills. Work indicates progress toward a goal.

Ladder: A means to go deeper within your mind. Notice if you are walking up or down the ladder and into which parts of your home/building you are entering. If you use a ladder to climb to the attic, you are moving into your superconscious mind.

Lake: Emotional life experiences. Since a lake is usually more placid than a river, this indicates you are experiencing emotional peace. However, this can also indicate stagnancy if the water is stagnant. You will need to examine your life to determine which description relates to you.

Lamp: A tool of your mind to create greater awareness and clarity. There may be some aspects of your thinking that you need to shed some light on.

Land: See *Earth*.

Laundry: Washing your clothes indicates you recognize the need to give care and attention to how you are expressing yourself to other people.

Law: You are aware that there may be consequences for your actions. You are looking at what would be the cause and effect outcomes of certain actions. You may also be coming to a greater understanding of your karma. You will benefit from studying and applying the "Universal Laws" in your life.

Leash (for a pet): A mental tool to keep your habit in check and under control.

Legs: Tools to cause motion in your life. You cause motion in your life by pursuing your goals and creating. If your legs are injured or not moving fast enough in the dream, then you need to be patient and practice visualizing your end goal to help you get there. If the legs are paralyzed, you may not be setting goals and hence cannot move. To move forward in life we need to set a goal, make a commitment, and take action.

Library: If you dream of a library, you have access to all of the wisdom of people around the world. A library is also the Universal Mind, where people are psychically connected. This is what enables you to know who is calling before you pick up the phone. It reveals you were in a state of mind where you could tap into the many ideas and thoughts of people around the world. This is also known as the Akashic Records that hold knowledge from the past.

License: Recognition of a competency. You may have a license to drive or practice holistic medicine. The license indicates a competency has been demonstrated in a skill that you possess. It may also represent a belief or attitude that gives you permission to do something like receive love from others.

Light: Awareness. In contrast, darkness symbolizes a lack of awareness. If you are always dreaming of life happening in daylight, it means that you are aware of what you think. If your dreams are dark, it means that there is a lack of awareness in your life about what you think and your direction in life.

Liquor: This induces a mental state where you have given up your will and control. If you are drunk, you have suppressed your thinking and logic skills and, therefore, cannot reason.

Lock: Tool within the mind to close or shut off a part of yourself. A locked door indicates you have closed your mind to certain ways of thinking.

Lotus Flower: See *Religious Symbol*.

Machine: Tool of the mind. Identify the function of the machine to understand what mental skill you are using. If you dream of a machine that helps process food, this relates to your ability to process knowledge.

Magic: Creation occurs without awareness of how it works. You believe your abilities happen without your control or effort. This is a misconception and reveals you are not aware of your abilities. You would benefit from studying the mind and visualization. You will see that nothing happens without you causing it.

Maid: Aspect of yourself that is devoted to maintaining order and purity in your thoughts.

Makeup: You are attempting to enhance or change your self-expression in a temporary, superficial fashion. It would benefit you to note your level of self-esteem and confidence. If you determine there is a challenge in this area, you will benefit by engaging in permanent methods of building your self-esteem, such as with self-respect and love.

Mansion: You see your mind as expansive and valuable.

Map: You are looking for direction in your life. You are aware there are many possible ways to reach a goal, and the mind can show you the different ways you can attain that goal or destination.

Market: A market is a place where you recognize how you want to use your energy and place your value. If you purchase something, you have seen value in it. For example, if you buy food, you value knowledge.

Marriage: Commitment to the inner self. When you marry someone, you commit to supporting and loving that person. This is the commitment you made to your inner self before entering the body. When marriage occurs in a dream you are committing to a union with your whole self.

Mask: The way you hide your true identity. Ask yourself what you do not want others to see and begin to change that part of yourself, or seek to understand the shame you feel about this part of yourself. Acceptance is the key to feeling good about yourself.

Meditation: The act of listening to and observing the inner self.

Meeting: The act of bringing various aspects of yourself together to share ideas. This creates a coordination of effort within your mind.

Menu: The variety of choices of knowledge available to you. You realize that you he have a choice about what you want to learn.

Microscope: A tool of the mind that allows you to see something that was hidden from you. Your new magnified vision relates to your enhanced skill of perception. Perhaps you recently discovered some personality flaws in someone you previously thought was perfect. This also relates to zooming in to the little details of life.

Military: Many aspects of yourself that are prepared to cause change at any time. Since the chief purpose of a military is to attack people or defend against attackers, it represents your ability to change something in your life or to preserve a way of life. The military also represents the practice of discipline in your life.

Mirror: A tool of the mind to see yourself clearly. Your dreams are a mirror of your consciousness, just as meditation and other spiritual practices can reflect your soul to you.

Miscarriage: A new idea or thought has been rejected by you. When a woman has a miscarriage, it indicates her body was not strong enough or prepared to carry the baby. In a dream it reveals you did not feel prepared to carry out this new idea or thought form. You need to fortify your mind and get mentally strong before taking on new ideas.

Money: Self value. If you dream of being rich, it symbolizes that you have discovered ways that you are valuable. If you dream of being poor, it indicates you will benefit by doing things to boost your self-value, like setting goals and accomplishing them and providing valuable service to others.

Monster: An aspect of yourself that is unknown to you and potentially dangerous or deadly. The monster usually represents some fear you feel you cannot control. It would benefit you to engage in activities that give you a sense of control over your life.

Moon: The moon brings light to the dark night sky. This signifies you have shed light on a problem or issue that was unclear. The awareness came from your inner self or subconscious mind.

Mountain: Challenge or obstacle in one's life. If you are climbing a mountain, it symbolizes you are currently working through a challenge. A mountain may also represent a lofty goal that has been set.

Movie: Use of imagination. The type of movie you are watching reveals how you are using your imagination. A movie about death shows you are imagining ways to cause change in yourself. A comedy shows that you are imagining having more fun in your life.

Mud: This indicates you are stuck in some situation. You need to get unstuck by processing the experience with the help of a counselor or friend.

Murder: The action of forcing a change. If you are murdering someone, identify the qualities associated with the person being killed to understand what part of yourself you are changing. If you dream of being murdered, it represents that you do not feel in control of the changes happening in your life. There is a need to calm your mind and recognize that creations take time to mature. Keep taking steps forward but relax and stop trying to force things to happen.

Museum: A place in your mind where you appreciate what has been created and learned in your past. The many valuable items in a dream museum are all of the abilities and skills you have learned, such as reading and writing. A museum reflects that you have been exploring and appreciating what you have built within.

Music: Harmony. You can choose music based on how you feel and the type of mood you want to induce. Likewise, you can create various forms of inner harmony. If you want inner stillness, you may obtain that through meditation. You may prefer the harmony that results from using your imagination to create a beautiful painting.

Naked: Openness and honesty. If you try to hide your nakedness, you are ashamed or embarrassed about your honesty. Perhaps during the day you said something you regret and want to hide your thoughts from others. However, if you are comfortable with your naked body, you have reached a point of being comfortable sharing yourself and your truth with others.

Nature: Subconscious existence. Nature is fertile ground where plant life grows. Your mind is the fertile ground where thoughts and ideas grow. It feels peaceful and good to be in nature, just as it feels good to connect with your subconscious mind.

Neck: Your neck connects your head with the rest of your body and represents your ability to take action (body) on your thoughts (head). A neck problem indicates you are stuck in your head and having difficulty integrating your ideas into your life. Your throat is related to will and communication while the cervical part of your spine relates to goals and ideals.

Night: Night can indicate a lack of awareness, or it can reflect your focus on assimilation and rejuvenation. It is a time of the daily cycle for recharging your batteries.

Nightmare: A nightmare reflects that you were in a state of fear and feeling out of control during the day. You feel things are happening to you that are out of your control, which often feels scary. A nightmare also indicates that a change needs to take place within yourself. Nightmares can often be traced back to themes that showed up in your dreams earlier, but no action was taken in these areas of your life. The message then becomes more intense and graphic until you consider it to be a nightmare.

Office: Place in your life where you are being productive and using your thoughts and actions to create something.

Oil: Energy that has much value and potential for you. Oil can be converted into gasoline for cars or used for many other beneficial purposes.

Opponent: Aspect of yourself that is in conflict with another part of yourself. To end the inner competition/conflict, you need to make this opponent your friend by cooperating rather than fighting.

Orphan: Seeing yourself as not having a foundation or inner roots. You have no connection to or awareness of your higher self (mother or father in the dream).

Outer Space: The expansive nature of the mind. Research shows that we use only 2-3% of our mind's power. If you travel to outer space in a dream, you have realized where and how you can access this unused potential. The expansiveness of outer space also represents the expansiveness of the superconscious mind.

Painting (artwork): Symbolizes the use of imagination and visualization.

Party: Your state of mind is focused on enjoying life. Depending on the type of party, you may be celebrating an accomplishment or a milestone.

Passport: Symbolizes your ability to access many different parts of the mind and ways of thinking. If the passport is for a specific country, identify your thoughts about that country. This will reveal the type of thinking you want to access. Your passport is your key to different ways of thinking.

Path: The direction you are moving in life. If you are walking the path and enjoying the scenery, you are moving towards your goal at a slow pace, yet with enjoyment. As Ralph Waldo Emerson said, "Do not go where the path may lead; go instead where there is no path and leave a trail."

Pentacle: See *Religious Symbol.*

Pentagram: See *Religious Symbol.*

People of various professions: Aspects of yourself that serve a particular function or role. Identify the function of the profession to understand what aspect of yourself it is reflecting. A nurse reflects the part of yourself that heals the mind. A banker would reflect a part of yourself that recognizes and manages the value that you see in yourself.

People: Aspects or qualities of yourself. Some yogis believe we have 144 parts that comprise who we are. Each person who appears in your dream represents one or more of these aspects or qualities. Think of one or two qualities that you associate with that person. This will reveal the part of yourself you expressed. People you know symbolize familiar aspects of yourself that can be easily identified. Unfamiliar people are parts of yourself you don't know. If you have frequent dreams with unfamiliar people, it means that there is a lack of awareness about your thoughts and attitudes. Knowing your thoughts is the first step in understanding yourself and the world around you. You will benefit from self-exploration through meditation and sciences such as astrology or numerology to gain deeper insights into yourself.

Pets: Habits. Domestic animals, such as dogs and cats, need to be analyzed on a personal level. Ask yourself what your pet represents to you. In many cases it is unconditional love. If you have a pet that performs a specific function, such as a dog that herds cattle, you were focused on using habits to improve your efficiency in life.

Phone: Tool for communication. You were communicating with your inner self or telepathically with another person.

Photograph: Memory. You have had an experience that is important to you and you wanted to remember it. The people in the photograph, if there were any people present, represent qualities of yourself.

Pills: Pills symbolize a tool that can heal your mind or body help you avoid your thoughts. You must identify the type of pills to determine which is occurring. A pill to take away pain is a way you are shutting down part of your mind to avoid your experiences. Pills that alter a person's consciousness symbolize a lack of will power, but in certain circumstances can also indicate an opening of consciousness.

Play: You are using your life experiences for enjoyment. Depending on the type of play involved, it can be considered a form of imagination. Studies show that children who are allowed to play a lot during their childhood develop strong imaginations.

Play (theater): Use of imagination. See movie.

Poison: The recognition of a thought or idea that is harmful to the state of your mind. When you poison another person, you are poisoning yourself since the other person is an aspect of you. If someone else is poisoning you, you feel a part of yourself is harming you.

Police: Disciplined aspects of yourself that help you stay within certain boundaries for your benefit. Police enforce the Universal Laws, such as cause and effect.

Pool: State of emotional enjoyment. The function of a pool is to provide fun and relaxation in a safe environment; hence, it reflects you are using your life experiences for fun. The water in the pool represents your emotional experiences. It may benefit you to ask why you are in a pool instead of the ocean. The pool allows you to play it safe, so there may be a fear associated with engaging in more expansive emotional life experiences.

Poverty: You see yourself as worthless and incapable of creating what you desire. It would benefit you to practice spiritual disciplines and set goals so that you can build your self-confidence and realize your power.

Praying: You are communicating with your higher self, or the Creator. Pay attention to what you are praying for, and this will reveal your deepest desires. Praying is a sign that you recognize your inner self is more powerful than your limited conscious mind.

Priest: Aspect that keeps the attention focused on spirituality and practices spiritual disciplines.

Prison: You think you are limited or stuck in your current life circumstances. You have built false limitations, based on your beliefs. You would benefit by surrounding yourself with expansive, positive thinkers, and joining a group or cause that will allow you to get your attention off yourself and devote yourself to a greater cause.

Protester: People protesting in a dream represent parts of yourself that are against what you are doing. Often when we make changes, there are parts of ourselves ingrained in the old way of doing things that will protest the change. Listen to what the protesters are saying to learn why those parts of yourself are not happy. It would benefit you to find a way to rally support from all aspects of yourself to avoid the turmoil caused by protesters. You can do this by making a list of the positive benefits you will receive by making the change or choice.

***Purse*:** Symbolizes how you view your identity and self-value. If you have lost your purse, you have forgotten your value, and hence are out of touch with your true identity. Your true identity is light and love, which is incredibly valuable.

***Puzzle*:** You are engaged in problem-solving. The answer to any question is found in the root cause, which is thought. You need to start at the point of cause (your thoughts) and trace your line of thinking to the current problem. When you put all the thoughts together, which is symbolic of putting all the puzzle pieces together, you see the full picture. The puzzle of life is like the web of karma that we weave each day through our thoughts and actions.

***Race (contest)*:** You are recognizing your competitive nature. You are viewing certain life events and circumstances with the desire to come out ahead. When you have this dream, keep in mind that all of the competitors are parts of yourself. Also, realize that there is more to life than being ahead of those around you.

***Radio*:** You are using your mind to receive messages from your inner self or telepathically from another person. Searching for a particular radio station means that you are directing your mind to hear a particular message.

***Rain*:** Water is essential to the human body as experiences are essential to the mind. Therefore, water or rain symbolizes emotional experiences. Rain means you are aware of the many different types of emotional experiences in your life. You are aware that you cannot avoid the emotional experiences because you are immersed in them. Depending on the amount of rain, you may also be feeling that your emotional life experiences are very intense and overwhelming. If this is the case, you need to assimilate your emotions every day and learn from them. The way you respond to the rain reveals how you respond to your emotional life experiences. Do you run from the rain, or do you enjoy it and sing in the rain?

Railroad Tracks: A course for a group or organization to follow. This keeps the organization focused on its goal or purpose. This is similar to a road or path.

Rape: You feel that something is being forced upon you. You have imagined something, and the subconscious is attempting to give it to you, and yet you are rejecting it.

It is important to identify who is doing the raping. If you are raping someone, it shows you are trying to force yourself to believe an idea or be a certain way. Sometimes this occurs when we have an unhealthy desire to impress other people. If you dream that you are being raped, it represents that you think you are being forced to be a certain way or accept a particular situation. If you dream of rape happening to people other than yourself, then you are objectively viewing this action taking place within you.

You will benefit by studying the process of visualization. The last step in this process involves accepting the creation. Once you have harmonized with what you have created, it is easier to start fresh and create something new. Also, be aware that the subconscious mind will create a fear with the same attention as a desire. Be diligent in keeping your attention on your desires instead of giving attention to what is not wanted in your life.

Recorder (tape, digital): Memory. Notice what you are recording in the dream to know what you desire to remember. An audio recording is a memory of something that you have heard.

Refrigerator: Tool within the mind to preserve knowledge and keep it fresh until you need it. One example of this is how the mind converts short-term memories into long-term memories. This helps us preserve lessons learned for use much later.

Religious Holiday: You are celebrating your spirituality. It is also the recognition of a spiritual accomplishment.

Religious Symbol: Tool to help direct your mind toward spiritual thinking and awareness.

Restaurant: You are in a state of mind to choose and receive knowledge. The money that you spend at the restaurant indicates the value that you see in this. The type of food that you are eating and the caliber of the restaurant indicate your perception of the quality of the knowledge that you are receiving.

Ring (wedding): Symbolizes commitment. When you marry, you are committing to live your life cooperatively with another person. When you took on a body, you agreed to use your conscious mind cooperatively with your subconscious mind to learn and create. A ring that is worn for fashion purposes reveals a commitment to valuing yourself. A graduation ring indicates you fulfilled a commitment to learn something.

Riot: State of mind where there is a great sense of upheaval and discontent. Notice what else is going on in the dream to determine what the unrest is related to. It would benefit you to create a list of goals and move toward those rather than focus on what you do not like in your life.

River: Emotional life experiences flowing in a set direction.

Road: The direction you are moving in life. If you are driving, this indicates you are moving at a rapid rate to your destination. A curvy or bumpy road indicates you are encountering some challenges along the way.

Running: The action of causing motion. If you are easily able to run in your dream, it means that you are easily able to cause forward movement in your life.

Sailing: Making the most of your emotional life experiences by purposefully directing your thoughts. You are actively harnessing the power of your thoughts (wind) to move through emotional life experiences.

Sand: Sand is often found at the boundary between land and water. Water is related to emotions. Sand is not fertile for most plants. Plants relate to developing thoughts. Therefore, sand is a part of your mind not fertile for developing your thoughts.

Scale: A tool to measure how you are using the knowledge that you have received. If the scale shows you have gained weight, it signifies that you have taken in more knowledge than you can use. Are you being a workshop junky, taking in more information that you can apply? If the scale reflects weight loss, then you have been starved for learning to some extent. Perhaps it is time to release some old knowledge that no longer serves you. Try to find a balance by using everything that you learn and taking in only as much as you can immediately apply.

School: You are focused on learning. If you are an adult and you dream of being in grade school, this can also indicate you are stuck in old ways of thinking and need to mature mentally. Going back to an earlier learning cycle, like going back to high school, can also indicate you are focused in the past. Recognize where you are on your path of personal growth and achievement.

Screaming: Screaming is something you may do when experiencing a powerful emotion often such as fear. You are reacting out of fear rather than using your mind to respond in a way that will produce a solution. You will benefit by meditating and engaging in creative problem-solving to determine how to respond to your life events.

Sea Animals: Underwater life represents habits that are unconscious and usually emotional in nature.

Seasons: Cycles in your life. Spring is a time when you are starting new projects and ideas (planting phase). Summer indicates you are enjoying working on your ideas and watching them grow. Fall is when you are focused on enjoying the fruits of your labors. Winter reflects a quiet time for you to go within to listen and connect with your inner self.

Senior Citizens: Aspects of yourself that have experience and wisdom.

Sexual Intercourse: You are harmonizing and connecting with a part of yourself. You are loving and enjoying a part of yourself, represented by the person you are having intercourse with; therefore, you have the possibility of creating something beautiful. If your dream sex partner is someone you describe as disciplined, then you are embracing that quality and using it to create something in your life. It might be helpful for you to describe your sexual partner in one or two words to understand this part of yourself better.

Ship: Represents an organization that offers you powerful emotional life experiences. This organization may be more experiential than mental, such as a hiking club. It may also provide a rich emotional experience since a ship sails on water. One example may be a service organization for the homeless.

Shoe: This symbolizes how you express your spiritual foundation (feet). A large heavy boot indicates you are hiding or protectin your spirituality. An open sandal signifies a more revealing attitude about your spirituality. A dirty worn-out shoe reveals a lack of care and concern for how you express your spirituality.

Shopping: This is the action of investing yourself in something and valuing an aspect of yourself or your life. Determine what you are purchasing to understand what you are currently valuing. If you are buying food, you are investing in knowledge. If you dream of buying clothes, you are investing in your self-expression.

Shower: You are purifying your mind of the day's thoughts, feelings and activities. Another way to describe this is "self-cleansing." Most people feel better after a shower, as well as when they purify or clean away thoughts, feelings and activities that can mentally weigh them down.

Skeleton: Represents the structure of the mind. You are becoming aware of what is beneath your ego and personality, and can see you have a structure that is the foundation for your mind.

Skies: Tools that aid you to move through stagnant emotional life experiences very quickly. It also can be a tool you use to gain more enjoyment as you move through life.

Sky: The vastness and expansiveness of the sky symbolizes the most expansive part of your mind, the subconscious and superconscious mind. When you dream of looking at the sky, you are connecting with the highest and wisest part of yourself.

Slow Motion: If you are only able to move in slow motion in the dream, it indicates you are running around without a clear goal in your life. You desire to move forward to attain a goal, but you are not able to do so. It will benefit you to identify where you want to go in life and the necessary steps to get there. If you want to change jobs, you must decide what type of job you desire, then visualize your dream job, update your resume, and begin searching for new positions. It may also indicate a lack of coordination in making a change in your life.

Snake: Habits that can be potentially dangerous. The habits usually relate to the way you create in your life. Since our kundalini (creative energy) is so precious, the snake holds a special significance in many cultures. The actions of the snake will reveal how you use your energy. You would benefit from connecting with your higher self to determine the best way to use your creative energies.

Snow: Stagnant emotional life experiences that have made life heavy for you. You need to see what thinking patterns have gotten you in a rut and create new expansive thoughts.

Soap: A tool to help you purify or change negative thoughts and experiences that have accumulated in your mind.

Soldier: A disciplined aspect of yourself that is prepared and trained to cause change.

Spaceship: A tool used to access the inner realms of your mind, such as the subconscious and superconscious. You have become aware that you can now access these inner dimensions. One method of doing this is through the regular practice of meditation.

Sports: You see life is a game that can be fun and/or competitive. You recognize that you need discipline, coordination and a cooperative attitude in order to win in life. The type of sport and how you play it will give you insights into how you see life and how you play the game of life.

Spouse: Aspect that you are committed to, usually your inner self.

Spring: See *Seasons.*

Stairs: You are aware of moving from one state/level of your mind to another. For example, when you go to sleep at night, you move your awareness from your conscious to your subconscious mind. When you meditate, you can move from your conscious to your subconscious or superconscious mind.

Star: A point of awareness that can guide you to a new understanding.

Star of David: See *Religious Symbol.*

Stealing: Taking from yourself. If you dream of stealing or being stolen from, you are taking from yourself in some way. What does this mean? It means you are negating something good within you; thus, you are taking from yourself. If you negate your talents, you are denying your self-worth.

Store: A place in mind where tools and knowledge are available to aid you. You must have money (self-value) in order to make use of these tools. It is a great feeling to know that whatever you need is available to you if you believe in yourself and your ability to create what you desire. If you lack the money necessary to purchase something in your dream, you need to re-affirm your value with positive affirmations.

Storm: Turbulence and confusion within yourself. You may be having emotional or mental challenges that feel overpowering and scary. If heavy rain is involved, your confusion is caused by overwhelming emotional life circumstances. High winds are turbulent thoughts and confusion. A storm can do damage, just as negative or turbulent thoughts can wear you down and lead you to states of mental anguish or depression. It will benefit you to face your problems and ask for help from your inner self before going to bed.

Street: Similar to a highway, a street represents the direction you are moving in life. Because you typically must drive slower on a street that on a highway, you are moving at a slower pace to reach your goal.

Student: Aspect of yourself that is focused on learning.

Suicide: You cannot find a solution to your problems, so you choose to run away from the learning by ending the experience. You are not valuing your life experiences and have lost touch with your true self, which is eternal. You are only identifying with your temporary physical self and problems. You will benefit from studying the Universal Laws, the law of karma, and the tools of the mind so you can learn how to solve your problems.

Suitcase: This is a tool of the mind used to carry and organize your various types of self-expression (clothing). If you are carrying a suitcase, it reveals you want to be prepared to express yourself appropriately, depending on where you are. For example, if you live in Alaska and are traveling to Hawaii, your heavy clothing will not be appropriate in Hawaii, and so you bring different clothes. Likewise, the way you express yourself in a formal meeting at work is different than how you express at a family party.

Summer: See *Seasons*.

Sunshine: The sun is the most powerful source of light, so it symbolizes the most powerful light inside us-our spirit that resides in the superconscious mind. Most people feel good when they see the sun shining and feel its warmth just as we feel good when we connect with the guidance of our spirit or higher self.

Surgery: You are in the process of correcting thoughts and attitudes that are harmful to your body and/or mind, such as excessive worry. Identify the area of the body that is undergoing surgery to determine what thoughts are in need of removal or correction. Eye surgery indicates a problem with perception, and hand surgery indicates a problem with expressing your life purpose.

Swimming: You are using your daily emotional life experiences for fun, relaxation and enjoyment. Swimming for fitness purposes indicates using your emotions to become a stronger, healthier person.

Sword: Tool to cause change in your life.

Taiji (yin and yang): See *Religious Symbol*.

Tardiness: When you arrive late to places, it reveals a belief that you should be further along in life than you are. If there is a feeling of anxiety associated with your dream, then you are also anxious about your status and position in life. For example, you may have a Bachelor's degree and feel you should have a Master's degree. It would benefit you to accept where you are and enjoy the process of learning and growth rather than the arrival at your destination. When you feel you need to be further along in life, this is a signal to be at peace in the present moment.

Teacher: Aspect committed to teaching and learning. This is an aspect of yourself that has authority with an understanding(s).

Teeth: Tools to process the knowledge you receive. If you dream that your teeth are falling out, it means that you are feeling overwhelmed by what you have learned and are having a difficult time processing it. It may also mean you are neglecting what you knows. For example, a man in a new job that is having difficulty learning all the new tasks may dream of his teeth falling out. You will benefit from focusing on each activity during the day and quieting your mind so you can absorb and assimilate new information.

Telephone: A tool for inner and/or outer communication. Notice who you are speaking with, and this will tell you the aspect of yourself with whom you are communicating. It will benefit you to practice daily meditation so you can receive the messages. A telephone in a dream can indicate a need to reveal your thoughts to other people.

Television: You are using your mind to receive messages from your inner self or telepathically from another person. It also represents the way you are using your imagination. Your ability to tune into a particular channel indicates your ability to imagine different things, or tune into different messages.

Temple (shrine): See *Church*.

Test: You are evaluating what you have learned. If there is anxiety involved, you may feel you are not prepared for life and are having difficulty learning from your experiences. You may feel that you are not as far along in your growth as you would like.

Texting: You are communicating with an aspect of yourself or telepathically with someone else. This type of communication requires some skill and coordination. Notice what the text message says in order to heed the message.

Theater: Symbolizes a state of mind where you are exercising your imagination. In a theater actors can try on different roles. This is where you are using your imagination to experience different ways of being before you make a commitment to one.

Thief: Aspect of yourself that devalues you and takes from you. For example, if you criticize yourself, this is a way of devaluing and taking from yourself.

Ticket (admission): You have acquired a mental tool that allows you to gain access to different aspects of your mind, such as your ability to learn and/or focus. A ticket to a movie reveals you are able to access your imagination.

Ticket (traffic): You are being reminded by a disciplined part of yourself (usually a police officer) that you have not obeyed your body signals and, therefore, needs to remember to place more value on your body.

Time: Time reveals your attention is on how much you have learned. The passage of time in a dream indicates that growth is occurring. Time is an illusion that you perceive and measure according to the amount of joy, fear, boredom or learning you experience. The question, "What time is it?" translates to "How much have I learned up to this point in my life?"

Toilet: A tool in the mind to help you release useless and unwanted thoughts, and feelings.

Tools: Mental qualities or skills that help you move through life.

Tornado: Since wind represents the movement of your thoughts, this overpowering wind signals you are confused and having difficulty controlling your thoughts. Strive to identify what is occurring in your life that may be causing you confusion or inner conflict. As you resolve these issues, this dream will cease.

Town: A state/place of mind. Identify your thoughts and judgments about the town to understand the state of mind this dream is reflecting. A town you view as overcrowded reflects a state of mind that is busy and noisy with mental chatter. A small town with few people can indicate a bored state of mind.

Toys: Tools of the mind to help you access your imagination. Toys are a source of play, which aids you to use your creative mind for enjoyment.

Train: A group or organization with a particular goal or destination.

Trash: You are aware that you must eliminate unnecessary thoughts and/or attitudes that no longer serve you. If the trash contains fresh food, you are wasting beneficial knowledge; however, if it contains other useful items, it can indicate waste in other areas of your life.

Trees: Thoughts developing in your subconscious mind. Trees reflect your growth over a long period of time; hence, they are ideas that have strength. If the trees in your dream are very healthy, your thoughts are positive and causing growth within you.

Tsunami: You are feeling extremely overwhelmed by life events that have the potential to cause major changes within you. Water represents your emotional energy, so your emotions are overwhelming you.

Universe: You have become aware of the expansive nature of your mind and realize there is still much untapped mental power that can be explored and utilized for your benefit.

University: You are focused on learning.

Vacation: Just as you can go on a vacation, you can also take a mental vacation. When you are on vacation in a dream, you have put aside your normal daily thoughts for a while. Other factors in the dream will reveal if you want to avoid thoughts, need rejuvenation, or want to break a habitual way of thinking. Just as a vacation can be physically beneficial for our health, putting aside negative thoughts for a while can be beneficial for the mind.

Vacuum Cleaner: Tool within your mind to remove unproductive thoughts and attitudes.

Victory: You have used your mind to overcome a challenge and reach a goal. There is a sense of satisfaction and excitement due to the achievement.

Video camera: Using your memory. Also, use of the imagination.

Volcano: There is great expansion occurring within your mind, symbolized by the fire and lava. If there is an explosion, its force signifies there are changes you have been working on for a long time. As these changes manifest, there is great excitement and a release of energy that has built up over a long period of time.

Wall: The expression, "I've come up against a wall," explains this symbol which signifies some limit or obstacle you are facing. You need to examine your thinking to see what limitation you have created in your mind. Since a house represents your mind, a wall in a house signifies you have closed yourself off from some part of your mind. If you are feeling stuck, perhaps you have put up a wall to the creative part of your mind.

Wallet: A place in your mind where you store your value and identity. A wallet in a dream reveals you value your identity.

War: You are making major changes in your life that are affecting many areas of your existence. War indicates an internal conflict between two or more aspects of yourself.

Washing Machine: Mental tool used to clean and improve the way you express yourself to others.

Water: Your emotions. Notice the way water is portrayed in the dream to understand your emotional state. If you are drowning in water, you are feeling overwhelmed. If you are happily swimming in a pool, this signifies you are in a positive emotional frame of mind and enjoying positive emotions. Your drinking water signifies conscious life experiences. Your body needs water each day to stay healthy just as your mind needs to absorb experiences each day.

Weapons: Tools for change.

Weather: The condition of your thoughts. A sunny warm day signals positive thoughts focused on your higher self while an overcast day reveals you are out of touch with your higher self due to negative thoughts and/or a lack of awareness.

Weeds: Negative thoughts of doubt and fear are growing in your mind and interfering with your desires. You will benefit by putting your attention on only what you want to manifest in your life. Whatever you put attention on will grow.

Well: A deep place in mind where you can see the source or root cause of your emotional life experiences.

Wheel: A mental tool to propel you with ease of movement. The type of wheel describes where this is occurring. Car wheels indicate tools that help your body move quickly and easily from one location to another, stroller wheels allow movement of new ideas. A solitary wheel shows you have had an "aha" moment where you have figured out a way to think or do something faster and/or more easily as in the saying, "The wheels are turning in your head."

Wheel of Dharma: See *Religious Symbol*.

Wind: Thoughts in motion. Strong winds indicate turbulent thoughts.

Window: You can now see new possibilities or ways of thinking. These new possibilities may be due to the fact that you have learned to access new parts of your mind. A window is also a way to view one part of your mind from another.

Wings: Tools to create freethinking. You have discovered mental tools or ways of thinking that create freedom. Your mind can weigh you down or help you soar to new heights!

Winter: See *Seasons*.

Work: Symbolizes how you are using your creative and mental abilities to produce something in your life. Since you get paid for doing your job, work also indicates you are prepared to be valued for your efforts. A recurring dream where you repeat the tasks you completed at work reveals you may be habitually creating without imagination. After working at a routine job for a long period of time, some people find they are doing the tasks without thinking.

World: Your whole mind which includes your conscious, subconscious and superconscious mind.

X-Ray: Tool within yourself to understand the inner workings of your mind and the effects of your thoughts.

Zoo: Place in your mind where you can observe all your mental habits. You can learn your types of habits and how you continue to maintain those habits with certain thoughts and attitudes. You need to "let the animals out of the cage" by releasing the habits that cause you to feel limited and "caged up."

REFERENCES

Quotes:

Anais Nin quotation. Retrieved from online. Web. 18 April, 2014.
http://www.brainquote.com/quotes/authors/a/anais_nin.html_n.d.

Carl Jung quotation. Retrieved from online. Web. 18 April, 2014.
http://www.goodreads.com/quotes/840979-the-dream-is-the-small-hidden-door-in-the-deepest_n.d.

Carl Jung quotation. Retrieved from online. Web. 20 April, 2014.
http://www.notable-quotes.com/j/jung_carl.html.n.d.

Edward Counsel quotation. Retrieved from online. Web. 20 April, 2014.
http://www.notable-quotes.com/d/dreams_quotes.html.n.d.

Kahlil Gibran quote. Gibran, Kahlil, "The Prophet," Oxford, England: One World Publications, 1998. Book.

Friedrich Nietzsche quote. Nietzsche, Friedrich, "Beyond Good and Evil," Mineola: Dover Publications Inc., 1997 Book.

Napoleon Hill quote. Hill, Napoleon, "Think and Grow Rich," Meriden: The Ralston Society, 1937. Book.

Tommy Cooper quotation. Retrieved from online. Web. 18, April, 2014.
http://www.brainyquote.com/quotes/quotes/t/tommycoope189070.html_n.d.

INDEX

REM (rapid eye movement) 6, 7

Serotonin 7, 42, 53
Sex 22, 28, 47, 52, 101
Sexy 18, 51, 53
Sigmund Freud 2
Sleep talking 36, 37
Sleeping pills 7
Sleepwalking 6, 34, 36
Soul 1, 3, 10, 11, 67, 70, 81, 90
Spirituality 20, 55, 56, 65, 68, 70,
96, 99, 101
Spouse 103
State of mind 20, 24, 61, 63, 65, 68,
69, 70-72, 80-81, 84, 88, 94, 99,
108
Subconscious 4, 7, 9, 11, 32, 39,
57-59, 82, 92, 98, 103
Subconscious mind 10-15, 25, 26,
28, 29, 31, 33, 34, 40-42, 52, 53,
59, 76-80, 84, 91, 92, 98, 99, 102,
103, 108, 111
Superconscious mind 10, 11, 49,
59, 64, 70, 77, 87, 94, 102, 103,
105, 111

Teen 47
Teenage 47
Television 106
Thalamus 5, 6
Toilet 45, 107
Tryptophan 7, 8
Tyrosine 8

Universal symbol 20, 21

Visitation 29

ABOUT THE AUTHORS

Patrick and Kathryn Andries have over 20 years dedicated to studying and teaching about dreams. They write a monthly dream column for *Aquarius* online magazine. They are also the co-founders of the School of Intuitive Arts and Sciences where they teach metaphysical classes and workshops.

Patrick teaches people across the United States how to live happier, healthier and more prosperous lives through classes, workshops and individual health coaching sessions. He is a practitioner of intuitive breathing and an energetic healer. He is a graduate of DePaul University where he earned a degree in physics and biology. He later earned a teaching certificate. He also earned a certificate of advanced study in metaphysics through the School of Metaphysics.

Kathryn's books include *Soul Choices: Six Paths to Find Your Life Purpose*, *The Dream Doctor*, *The Big Desire*, and *Soul Choices: Six Paths to Fulfilling Relationships*. She also produced the video *Inside the California Missions*. She received a Bachelor of Arts degree in economics from the University of Michigan, and a holistic health practitioner degree from Body Mind College. She completed extensive studies in the intuitive arts at the Berkeley Psychic Institute, the School of Metaphysics, and the American Federation of Astrologers.

Other Books By Ozark Mountain Publishing, Inc.

Dolores Cannon
Conversations with Nostradamus,
    Volume I, II, III
Jesus and the Essenes
They Walked with Jesus
Between Death and Life
A Soul Remembers Hiroshima
Keepers of the Garden.
The Legend of Starcrash
The Custodians
The Convoluted Universe - Book One,
    Two, Three, Four
Five Lives Remembered
The Three Waves of Volunteers and the
    New Earth
Stuart Wilson & Joanna Prentis
The Essenes - Children of the Light
Power of the Magdalene
Beyond Limitations
Atlantis and the New Consciousness
The Magdalene Version
O.T. Bonnett, M.D./Greg Satre
Reincarnation: The View from Eternity
What I Learned After Medical School
Why Healing Happens
M. Don Schorn
Elder Gods of Antiquity
Legacy of the Elder Gods
Gardens of the Elder Gods
Reincarnation...Stepping Stones of Life
Aron Abrahamsen
Holiday in Heaven
Out of the Archives – Earth Changes
Sherri Cortland
Windows of Opportunity
Raising Our Vibrations for the New Age
The Spiritual Toolbox
Michael Dennis
Morning Coffee with God
God's Many Mansions
Nikki Pattillo
Children of the Stars
A Spiritual Evolution
Rev. Grant H. Pealer
Worlds Beyond Death
A Funny Thing Happened on the Way to
    Heaven
Maiya & Geoff Gray-Cobb
Angels - The Guardians of Your Destiny
Maiya Gray-Cobb
Seeds of the Soul
Sture Lönnerstrand
I Have Lived Before
Arun & Sunanda Gandhi
The Forgotten Woman
Claire Doyle Beland
Luck Doesn't Happen by Chance

James H. Kent
Past Life Memories As A Confederate
    Soldier
Dorothy Leon
Is Jehovah An E.T
Justine Alessi & M. E. McMillan
Rebirth of the Oracle
Donald L. Hicks
The Divinity Factor
Christine Ramos, RN
A Journey Into Being
Mary Letorney
Discover The Universe Within You
Debra Rayburn
Let's Get Natural With Herbs
Jodi Felice
The Enchanted Garden
Susan Mack & Natalia Krawetz
My Teachers Wear Fur Coats
Ronald Chapman
Seeing True
Rev. Keith Bender
The Despiritualized Church
Vara Humphreys
The Science of Knowledge
Karen Peebles
The Other Side of Suicide
Antoinette Lee Howard
Journey Through Fear
Julia Hanson
Awakening To Your Creation
Irene Lucas
Thirty Miracles in Thirty Days
Mandeep Khera
Why?
Robert Winterhalter
The Healing Christ
James Wawro
Ask Your Inner Voice
Tom Arbino
You Were Destined to be Together
Maureen McGill & Nola Davis
Live From the Other Side
Anita Holmes
TWIDDERS
Walter Pullen
Evolution of the Spirit
Cinnamon Crow
Teen Oracle
Chakra Zodiac Healing Oracle
Jack Churchward
Lifting the Veil on the Lost Continent of
    Mu

For more information about any of the above titles, soon to be released titles,
or other items in our catalog, write or visit our website:
PO Box 754, Huntsville, AR 72740
www.ozarkmt.com

Other Books By Ozark Mountain Publishing, Inc.

Guy Needler
The History of God
Beyond the Source – Book 1,2
Dee Wallace/Jarred Hewett
The Big E
Dee Wallace
Conscious Creation
Natalie Sudman
Application of Impossible Things
Henry Michaelson
And Jesus Said – A Conversation
Victoria Pendragon
SleepMagic
Riet Okken
The Liberating Power of Emotions
Janie Wells
Payment for Passage
Dennis Wheatley/ Maria Wheatley
The Essential Dowsing Guide
Dennis Milner
Kosmos
Garnet Schulhauser
Dancing on a Stamp
Julia Cannon
Soul Speak – The Language of Your
    Body
Charmian Redwood
Coming Home to Lemuria
Kathryn Andries
Soul Choices – 6 Paths to Find Your Life
    Purpose

For more information about any of the above titles, soon to be released titles,
or other items in our catalog, write or visit our website:
PO Box 754, Huntsville, AR 72740
www.ozarkmt.com